WHAT HAVE
WE LEARNED?

WHAT HAVE WE LEARNED?

Lessons for the Church in the Twenty-first Century

LYLE E. SCHALLER

Abingdon Press
Nashville

WHAT HAVE WE LEARNED:
Lessons for the Church in the Twenty-first Century

Copyright © 2001 by Abingdon Press

Library of Congress Cataloging-in-Publication Data

Schaller, Lyle E.
    What have we learned? : lessons for the church in the twenty-first century /
    Lyle E. Schaller.
        p. cm.
    Includes bibliographical references (p.).
    ISBN 0-687-04540-1 (alk. paper)
    1. Pastoral theology. I. Title.

BV4011.3 .S37 2001
253—dc21

                                                                00-045129

Scripture quotations, unless otherwise indicated, are from the *New Revised Standard Version of the Bible*, copyright 1989, by the Division of Christian Education of the National Council of the Churches of Christ in the United States of America.

01 02 03 04 05 06 07—10 9 8 7 6 5 4 3 2 1

MANUFACTURED IN THE UNITED STATES OF AMERICA

TO
AGNES

The Perfect Wife
Lover
Best Friend
Companion
Partner
Cheerleader
Mother
Student
Baker
Editor
Critic
Nurse
Advocate
Computer Operator
Gardener
Photographer
Grandmother
Electrician
Chef
Dietician
Author
Tailor
E-Mailer
Snow Remover
Diagnostician
Carpenter
Hostess
Chauffeur
Navigator
Bird Feeder
Sweetheart

CONTENTS

J- 1ST S

J- lost 4

Introduction

To make it easier to comprehend the world in which we live, we all divide that complex environment into smaller units. One system divides it into air, water, and land. Another into the earth, heaven, and hell. A third into children, youth, and adults. A fourth into Republicans, Democrats, and Independents. A fifth into books, magazines, and newspapers. A sixth into God, Jesus, and the Holy Spirit. A seventh into Protestant, Catholic, and Jew. An eighth into lower class, middle class, and upper class. A ninth into for, against, and no opinion. A tenth into alive, dying, and dead. An eleventh system divides the stages of a pregnancy into three trimesters. A twelfth divides the sermon or speech into three parts.

Hundreds of these systems for dividing the world into categories exist. Many use three categories.

In introducing the contexts of this book, I will divide the population into only two groups—optimists and pessimists. I will examine the institutional expression of the Christian faith in America, but will look out of two different windows.

As an optimist about the future of the Christian churches in America, I look at a glass that is more than half full. The pessimist sees a glass that is half empty.

The pessimist points to the numerical decline and aging of the membership in several mainline Protestant denominations and in a majority of Protestant congregations founded before 1960. As an optimist, I am impressed with the vitality, relevance, appeal to younger generations, and energy in so many of the new missions founded in the last quarter of the twentieth century (see chap. 1).

The pessimist points to various polls and surveys that report a decrease in the proportion of American adults in church on the typical weekend. The optimist (a) points out that these polls tend to provide less than an accurate picture of reality and (b) cites reports from congregations that actual worship attendance in Protestant congregations in the United States nearly doubled in the second half of the twentieth century.

The pessimist is discouraged by the difficulties encountered in renewing the old. The optimist is delighted with the successes in creating the new (see chap. 11).

The pessimist looks out and is distressed by the continued racial and nationality segregation in the churches. The optimist, who may be a white integrationist at heart, sees a society that affirms the right of self-determination (see chaps. 4 and 18).

Instead of lamenting the continued racial segregation in the churches, the optimist rejoices in the recent rapid increase in the number and variety of African American and Afrocentric megachurches. The pessimist points out that only a few of these are related to one of the mainline Protestant denominations with a western European religious heritage.

The pessimist is distressed by the ever increasing demands younger generations bring to the church. The optimist is delighted to see so many young adults in church and rejoices with those congregations that are both able and willing to offer people a range of attractive choices. The optimist also is pleased that these younger generations apparently believe the churches can be responsive to their needs (see chaps. 1 and 3).

The pessimist looks out and sees the continued increase

in the number of small congregations in the denomination. The optimist looks out and sees that increase in the number of large churches and points out that two dozen of those very large congregations include more worshipers on the typical weekend than a thousand of those small churches. What do you count? Institutions? Or worshipers? (See chap. 16.)

The pessimist is convinced that secularism and consumerism are ruining America. The optimist agrees with Robert Fogel that the United States is experiencing a new religious reawakening.[1]

The pessimist looks out and sees a decline in the moral standards of American society and concludes that the devil is alive and at work in this world. The optimist looks out at the transformations in the lives of individuals on a personal spiritual journey and celebrates the fact that God is alive and at work in the world. (See chap. 10 for one model.)

The pessimist points to the surveys that report that despite recent sharp increases in personal income, churchgoers still contribute the same proportion of their income to the church as they did a decade or two earlier. The optimist points to the large gifts from accumulated wealth that Christians are contributing to religious needs (see chap. 9).

The pessimist laments the declining interest in the churches in classical Christian music. The optimist is impressed by how enthusiastically younger generations are responding to this new Christian music and to the creativity expressed in participatory worship (see chap. 13).

The pessimist is discouraged by the number of youth who drop out of church shortly after confirmation. The optimist is thrilled by the teenage "radical Christians" who are having such an impact on the student body in so many high schools.

The pessimist feels threatened by the rapid growth in the number of churchgoers who are on-line. The optimist is delighted with the opportunities the World Wide Web has created for congregations to proclaim the gospel of Jesus Christ to a larger constituency (see chap. 14).

The pessimist is depressed by the inability of the traditional women's missionary organization to attract women born after 1960. The optimist is surprised and delighted by the large number of young women who are enthusiastic and regular participants in those ministries tailored to address the personal and spiritual concerns of adults on a religious pilgrimage.

The pessimist feels threatened by the growing influence of marketing and laments the resulting competition among the churches for future constituents. The optimist perceives competition to be a healthy stimulus to creativity, innovation, and accountability (see chap. 8).

The pessimist sees the rising level of demographic diversity as a challenge to uniformity. The optimist declares that the concept of federalism has taught Americans how to enjoy the benefits of diversity (see chap. 2).

The pessimist bemoans the growing impact of entertainment on American culture. The optimist responds by pointing out that Christianity is by definition an experiential religion (see chap. 7).

The pessimist laments the failure of congregations to cooperate in community outreach ministries. The optimist celebrates the community ministries of that growing number of strong congregations (see chap. 5).

The pessimist bemoans the increase in obesity. The optimist responds, "Replace those pews with chairs" (see chap. 12).

Finally, the pessimist and the optimist, while viewing the American church scene from two different perspectives, do agree that the role and responsibilities of the parish pastor are far more demanding today than was the case in the 1950s. The pessimist questions whether theological seminaries are equipped to prepare students to be effective parish pastors in the twenty-first century.

This optimist declares, "Let us not place unrealistic expectations on the seminaries.

"First of all, let us rejoice in the expanding role for the laity in what formerly were clergy-dominated religious institutions.

"Second, let us rejoice in the rapid proliferation of resources in recent years that are designed to help congregational leaders define what God is calling their church to be and to do in the years ahead. These resources include teaching churches, parachurch organizations, entrepreneurial individuals, publishing houses, and those regional judicatories that have concluded that their primary role is not to do ministry, but to help congregations succeed in their ministry" (see chap. 17).

While the task of serving as a parish pastor is far more demanding today than it was in the 1950s, the good news is that we have learned a lot during the past few decades on how "to do church better." Most of these insights and lessons were not available to the congregational leaders of 1955.[2]

This book represents an attempt to summarize a few slices of the wisdom, insights, and lessons that have been earned and learned in the past several years. They have been drawn from my working directly on their turf with approximately 4,000 congregations over a period of four decades, from 1960 to 2000. This optimist hopes that these illustrations will be of help to congregational leaders, both lay and ordained, to be more faithful and more effective in leading their church in the path God has chosen for that particular called-out community.

Lyle E. Schaller

Naperville, Illinois

May 2000

CHAPTER ONE
WHAT HAPPENED?

When I joined the staff here at First Church in 1957, I was fresh out of seminary and twenty-five years old," recalled a retired minister who had returned for the celebration of this congregation's sesquicentennial as a downtown church. At that time we were averaging well over 1,200 at worship, and that included hundreds of couples with young children. Many of our leaders represented the old guard who had been born before the turn of the century, but by the time I left in 1962 to lead my own church, most of our leaders came from the generations born after World War I. Two of our best leaders were my age.

"In 1950 there were seven mainline Protestant congregations meeting either in the downtown area or only a few blocks beyond. By the time I arrived in 1957, one had relocated to the southside. During my five years here, three more relocated to larger sites and constructed new facilities. Since we left, one of the three remaining downtown churches merged into a new mission it had started years earlier on the north side. That means only two of those seven are still here, and the other one is surviving thanks largely to a $3 million endowment fund.

"We moved out-of-state when we left here, and this is our first time back since 1975. I really have a difficult time understanding all the changes. When I joined the staff, this was the leading church in our denomination in the state. We were attracting well over two hundred new members year after year. We were the second largest Protestant congregation in the entire county. Yesterday I was told that the population of this county has more than doubled since the 1950s, but over half of the residents live outside the city. Most of the big churches today are farther to the west and the south, out on the edge of the city or in the suburbs. Last year, I am told, worship attendance here averaged slightly over four hundred, and only forty-seven new members were received. From what we've been told, the present staff is doing many of the things we did when I was here, but they're not getting the results we did."

Four miles southwest of First Church is the three-acre site that is the meeting place for Augustana Lutheran Church. This congregation was founded on what at the time was the far southwestern edge of this growing city in 1957. It was launched to reach and serve the families moving into the new houses being constructed on what had been farmland. At that time these houses on 60' x 120' lots sold for $17,000 to $21,000. Ten years later this parish was averaging nearly six hundred at worship. A decade after that, attendance plateaued at nearly a thousand and remained on that plateau until the late 1980s. The founding pastor retired in 1987, and the successor turned out to be a serious mismatch in terms of the gifts, skills, personality, priorities, and expectations he brought and what Augustana Church needed at that point in its history. He left after a tumultuous two years. The fourth senior pastor in Augustana history arrived two years ago. Last year this aging and numerically shrinking congregation reported a combined average worship attendance of 575 for the three weekend services. A new mission that Augustana sponsored in 1986 meets on a nine-acre site six miles to the west and last year averaged nearly seven-hundred at worship.

New Generations Bring New Expectations

While located in two different community settings, these two congregations have experienced several similar points of discontinuity with the past. The most significant point of discontinuity is that in 1957 both First Church and Augustana Lutheran focused their ministry primarily on adults born in the pre-1935 era. Both were exceptionally effective in reaching and serving the younger adults of the 1950s. Today most of the adults of 1957 can be found on golf courses or in retirement villages, cemeteries, nursing homes, columbariums, or smaller and numerically declining Protestant churches.

Their current successors, the generations born after 1965, bring a different set of expectations to church. What worked for the churches in reaching and serving the generations born before 1935 often is found to be somewhere between irrelevant and ineffective in ministries with younger generations.

Among the differences many of the younger generations bring are (1) new preferences in music; (2) a new set of criteria in choosing a church home as relevance, quality, and meaningful choices have moved ahead of geographical proximity, kinship ties, inherited nationality, and denominational loyalties; (3) stronger expectations that the church will "help us rear our children"; (4) a preference for participatory rather than presentation-type of worship services; (5) an assumption that a conveniently located and vacant parking space will be available at the end of every journey; (6) a far more relaxed dress code (this is more visible in the North and West than in the South); (7) a conviction that important policy questions will be decided locally rather than handed down by a distant and impersonal bureaucratic structure; (8) an expectation that every building designed to serve the general public will have clean, attractive restrooms conveniently located near the major entrance; (9) previous experiences that have taught them that every volunteer will receive the appropriate training before beginning to serve in a volunteer role; (10) a demand for more choices in worship, ministries with teenagers, adult learning opportunities, and volunteer roles; (11) a preference for an experiential approach to learning versus the traditional lecture format; (12) a high level of comfort with communication via projected visual imagery; (13) a preference for singing with the head held high rather than looking down into a book; (14) a strong preference for designated financial gifts rather than obligatory contributions to an organization where a distant group of decision makers will choose the ultimate recipients of those gifts; (15) a conviction that one's life should be organized primarily around meaningful relationships and individual choices rather than around obligations, duties, customs, and legalistic requirements; (16) a far greater probability that a couple is either (a) in an interdenominational or interfaith or intercultural marriage or (b) living together but not married; and (17) a greater willingness to travel five to fifteen miles each way to church two or three times a week.

In addition to those seventeen pieces of baggage, most of the members of these younger generations have been taught nine other lessons.

From Radio to Television to the Internet

Radio was the influential teacher that arrived on the scene in the 1920s and 1930s. Before the coming of radio, a day was divided into three parts—morning, afternoon, and evening. Radio taught people that time is divided into sixty-minute periods. The length for the Sunday morning worship service gradually shrank from an hour or two or three, more or less, to approximately one hour. Radio taught speakers how to address a largely passive and unseen audience. Eventually radio taught people that an

20

hour is divided into four fifteen-minute segments (not six ten-minute segments). This meant that congregations could schedule worship to begin on the quarter hour, for example, at 9:15 or 10:45 on Sunday morning. It also led many to believe that the choice was between a thirty-minute or a fifteen-minute sermon.

Radio also taught listeners that the appropriate musical accompaniment might include one person playing the piano or one person playing an organ and/or a performance-type of choir. Usually itinerant evangelists and preachers would be accompanied by their own pianist or organist in their travels.

Before the arrival of FM, radio also taught people that if the listener wanted to hear everything that was said, the listener had 100 percent of the obligation to listen carefully. Radio taught people to be quiet and passive listeners. Radio taught that oral and printed channels of communication are the best ways to communicate the gospel. Radio taught listeners that the visual imagery people seek will be largely the product of their own imagination. Radio taught that life is sequential. Radio confirmed the conviction that a well-organized sermon consists of an introduction, point one, point two, point three, and a conclusion. That continues to be excellent advice for anyone speaking to people born before the mid-1950s.

Then came television. For the first dozen or so years, television programming was conceptualized and designed largely by persons who had been trained in radio. Up through the 1950s, and perhaps even into the 1960s, television was radio with black-and-white moving pictures. It was not until 1963, for example, that the three major broadcast networks decided that an hour should be divided into two thirty-minute segments rather than four fifteen-minute segments. That decision was accompanied by the decision to expand the period for network news from fifteen to thirty minutes. Most of the viewers of black-and-white televi-

21

sion perceived what they saw on that small screen to be a fantasy world. It was a nice place to visit, but they lived in the real world.

Fantasy to Reality

Radio had helped to build a following for major league baseball. The fan could enjoy up-to-the-minute reporting on the progress of a game by listening to the radio. If one wanted to really enjoy a game, however, that required a trip to the ballpark. A few years later, radio helped to make World War II the most "popular" war in American history. Most of what the listeners heard on the radio or saw in the motion picture theaters about World War II from 1941 to 1945 was fantasy. It was a highly sanitized version of what war is all about. The Korean conflict was brought home to the American people in largely sanitized and patriotic black-and-white pictures as well.

Then came color television. The Vietnam war came into people's living rooms in living color, much of it red. These were not fantasy pictures. Viewers perceived those pictures to represent contemporary reality!

In the 1960s, and especially in the 1970s, television began to bring to viewers a new, more colorful, and dynamic version of a worshiping community. This was not fantasy. This became the new standard for comparison. Television raised the bar three or four notches in defining acceptable quality in communication, in worship, in teaching, and in physical facilities.

The remote control device also taught television viewers that 100 percent of the responsibility for grabbing and holding the attention of the viewer rested on the speaker, not the listener. This has transformed the pedagogical style of high school, college, and university teachers. At least a few have chosen to resign rather than accept that new responsibility.

Television taught that effective communication is one-to-one communication, not one person addressing a large and attentive crowd. Television taught that effective communication includes words, music, action, color, visual imagery, change of pace, emotion, humor, trust, and drama. Television taught people that the sermon should address the concerns of the listener. Television taught that effective communication can and should evoke a response from the viewer.

The television program *M*A*S*H* introduced the concept of a message with two alternating and concurrent story lines. That is a useful model when speaking to people born after 1950.

Radio taught the baseball fan to go to the ballpark to see the game played by men in gray-and-white uniforms. Television taught that you can have a better view from your living room as you watch the players in colorful uniforms.

In a few years the World Wide Web will make it possible for congregations in obscure locations to invite a global constituency to worship with them by watching their television screen (see chap. 14).

Television also created both the environment and the constituency for a new approach to corporate worship. A common result is that the intergenerational congregation schedules a traditional worship service with a predictable sequence for people reared in the radio culture and a nontraditional participatory worship experience for those reared in the world of color television. Even more common, however, are the congregations that schedule one or two worship services for Sunday morning with both designed on the 1952 radio model. The leaders spend the rest of the week wondering why that congregation is growing older and smaller.

From Studying to Experiencing

As you walk to the post office or the public library or through the park, how many boys in the ten- to fifteen-year-old age bracket do you see riding a bicycle? How many on a skateboard?

One of the most interesting trends of the 1990s was the emergence of a variety of extreme sports, such as skydiving, snowboarding, and base jumping, as well as a sharp increase in the number of rock climbers. Little League baseball, which is largely a passive sport, has a new rival called soccer. Soccer is a participatory game.

A parallel is the change in the way younger generations of churchgoers are being taught to respond to the call to support missions.

The past years brought a renewed interest in motivating believers to become active supporters of world missions. One approach was to invite missionaries on furlough to come and tell their story. One goal was to enable church members to understand more fully the need for missionary work. Another was to raise money for missions. In several denominations a concurrent strategy called for sending denominational leaders to visit foreign mission stations and, after returning, to share their experiences with their congregation. More recently, pastors were urged to visit mission fields themselves to enable them to inspire parishioners with a vision of the need for congregations to support foreign missions. An obvious part of that design was to increase financial support by congregations for denominational mission causes and to motivate pastors to lift up the need for more missionaries. The combination of affluence and easier travel produced the next stage, which called for lay volunteers to spend a week or two visiting several mission stations. When they returned, they usually served as enthusiastic advocates of world missions.

The newest stage emerged in the 1980s and blossomed in the 1990s. This new model is replacing the old model, which called for congregations to send money to another agency that would support missionary efforts in every part of the planet. This new model calls for a direct, "sister church" relationship between an American parish and a congregation in another country or even another part of the United States. One version calls for the suburban congregation to enter into a sister-church relationship with a congregation in the central city. Another calls for the suburban congregation to plant a new mission in the central city or an older suburb. A third version calls for a congregation to plant new missions in other states. A fourth version calls for the American church to enter into a sister-church relationship with a congregation in another country.

Instead of funneling resources through an intermediary, this last model calls for a direct relationship. (This appears to be part of a larger societal trend of eliminating what historically was called the "middle man.") This model calls for the "sending" churches to send **both** people and money to their sister church. The people go, not as tourists, but rather as partners in doing ministry.

The **big** unanticipated fringe benefit of this model is the impact of this experience on the lives of those volunteers in missions. Many volunteers describe it as a "life-changing experience" (see chap. 10).

These four paragraphs introduce what may turn out to be the greatest change in "how we do church in America" to come out of the twentieth century.

The change is from hearing, studying, watching, and observing to experiencing. One example is the evolution from the presentation-type of worship service to the participatory worship experience. A more common example is that the old organizing principle for youth groups of studying, learning, and discussing is being replaced by experiences and networking.

Currently the biggest debate over this change is in high schools. The teachers graduated from a college or university where the 1930s pedagogical system of listening to lectures, participating in discussion groups, writing book reports, reading assigned books, completing term papers, and being rewarded for individual performance dominated the educational process. That system was owned and operated by adults, most of whom were born before 1960.

Today's high school teacher walks into a classroom filled with fifteen-year-olds who have grown up with television, IMAX motion picture theaters, computers, camcorders, videotapes, and cell phones. They have mastered a small magical, handheld device that empowers them, without moving from their chair, to switch off any television program that fails to grab and hold their attention.

Instead of a spring break's being a vacation from school, it may be a nine-day trip to another region or another country. Retail trade has been transformed from a chore to an experience. Restaurants once were rated on the quality of their food. Now they are ranked by the experience they provide the diner. The teenager's ability to travel once was determined by access to public transportation. Now it is, "Shall we take your car or my mom's van?"

The teacher in that high school passes out a one-page printed sheet and explains, "We'll take a few minutes for you to read this, and then we'll discuss it." The translation is, "Let's return briefly to a world that began to disappear about the time you were born."

Younger generations have been taught that going to church, supporting missions, and discovering how the gospel of Jesus Christ can transform one's life has evolved from an obligation to a series of memorable and meaningful experiences. The road that brought worshipers to church in the 1950s may not be the road that will be chosen by those going to church in the twenty-first century!

The church-sponsored book study group was a relevant design for adults born before 1950. It is less effective with adults who recall, "I was able to graduate from high school without ever cracking open a book."

The Impact of Decentralization

In the 1950s the economic base of the central business district usually included city hall, the main post office, department stores, the first-run motion picture theaters, several big Christian churches, hotels, financial institutions, restaurants, the YMCA, an office-supply store, high-rent apartment buildings, a couple of five-and-dime variety stores, professional offices, a bookstore, and perhaps one or two county, state, or federal office buildings. Most of the workers or visitors to that central business district arrived via public transit. After arrival, many had to climb one or two flights of stairs to reach their destination.

The next few decades brought the decentralization of the urban economy. A greater reliance on the privately owned motor vehicle was both a cause and a consequence of decentralization.[1] Another cause was the price of land. One consequence was the relocation of hundreds of downtown congregations' meeting places from quarter-acre parcels of expensive land to three-acre sites that included room for a hundred or more parking spaces.

Another consequence of lower priced land was that the one-story suburban structure replaced the older norm of a two- or three- or four-story downtown building.

Decentralization plus affluence produced two other changes that have had a huge impact on church planning. In 1957 there were 805 privately owned motor vehicles for every 1,000 licensed drivers in the United States. At the beginning of the twenty-first century that ratio was 1,130 for every 1,000 licensed drivers. One cause and one consequence of that change is that the journey to work has become longer and longer. The longer that journey to work, the easier it is for people to accept a journey of five to ten to fifteen miles to church.

The combination of that longer journey with greater affluence means that twice as many vehicles are required to bring one hundred people to church as were needed as recently as 1970 (see chap. 12).

Growth Brings Competition

The population of that urban county served by First Church and Augustana Lutheran Church has more than doubled since 1957. That not only means new generations for the churches to reach and serve, but also many more people of all ages. The old assumption was that an increase in the population would result in an increased size for the congregations serving that community. "A rising tide lifts all the ships in the harbor" was a cliché of the 1960s that reinforced this assumption.

In retrospect we have learned that a significant increase in population attracts new missions. The result is greater competition among the churches for prospective future constituents. It has become clear that the rising tide does lift many of the ships in the harbor, but it also sinks those ships that were tightly tied to the traditions and customs of an earlier time (see chap. 8).

In late 1957 Augustana Lutheran Church was the second newest Protestant congregation in the county. Today it is among the older half. Many of today's members who joined back in the 1960s and 1970s are convinced that, "If we would do what we did here back when I was a new member, I'm sure we could attract a lot more young people." Several of the younger leaders who have joined during the past dozen years agree with the current senior pastor that the road this parish traveled so comfortably for thirty years is not the road that will take them into a happy tomorrow.

Several of the older pillars are absolutely horrified when one of these younger leaders points out, "We are living in a far more competitive environment for the churches than prevailed back when Augustana was founded." These old-timers point out that it is completely unchristian to even suggest that churches compete with one another.

Back at old First Church, however, this increased competition is accepted as a fact of life. One longtime member expressed it very clearly: "While I still believe it was the right thing for us to do, we did place a ceiling on our future when we funded three new missions. In 1952 we sent nearly a hundred members plus one of our pastors out to found what is now Bethany Church. Six years later we sent at least three dozen families and a pastor out to start what became Calvary Church. Our son and his wife and their children were one of those families. In 1963 we sponsored Hope Church. Today all three are larger than First Church. Each one has new buildings on a large parcel of land at a great location. I guess we thought we were planting new churches, but what we really were doing was planting the seeds of our own future decline. We created our own competition."

Each one of those three new congregations sponsored by First Church meets on a site that includes more than three hundred off-street parking spaces. Two meet in what are essentially one-story buildings. The oldest of the three has a two-story educational wing, but in all three the worship center is on the first floor. Two of the three have a full-size gymnasium.

The Consequences of Success

While the impact of this change has been felt more strongly in the North and the West than in the Southeast, perhaps the most rarely mentioned highly influential trend of the second half of the twentieth century was the success of the ecumenical movement. The old rhetoric called for Christian churches to emphasize what "distinguishes our religious traditions and teachings from the others." The 1950–75 era brought a new worldview. "Let us not focus on what separates us, but rather let's concentrate on what we have in common." One consequence was a series of denominational mergers. Another was widespread support for interdenominational councils of churches. A third was that the ecumenical movement created a fertile context for interfaith cooperation in the civil rights movement. A fourth consequence was more subtle. The generations who grew into adulthood during the second half of the twentieth century display limited interest in what separates one religious tradition from all others. That criterion for determining the distinctive identity of a congregation has been replaced by a new question: "Which congregation is prepared to respond to my personal and spiritual needs, to speak to me in terms of my personal faith journey, and to respond meaningfully to my needs at this stage of my life cycle?"

Church shopping has become the norm for younger adults dissatisfied with the religious tradition of their parents, with newcomers to a community, with persons in an interdenominational or interfaith marriage, and with adults and teenagers on a serious personal religious quest. The old barriers that limited the range of choices for church shoppers have been reduced by ecumenism. The combination of affluence; the rise of consumerism; the lengthening of the journey to work, to shop, and to recreation; and the disappearance of neighborhood-oriented institutions (motion picture theaters, grocery stores, physicians' offices, neighborhood elementary schools, barbershops, and taverns) has expanded the list of choices on that church shopping list.

Back in 1957, First Church identified two or three rivals as its chief competitors for prospective future members. Many of the community leaders in 1957 were invited by their peers to join other "shakers and movers" at First Church. Today their counterparts are scattered among a dozen or more congregations.

The New Kids on the Block

The biggest measurable religious change in most urban communities has been in the mix of Protestant congregations. In the 1950s most of the Protestant congregations were affiliated with one of two dozen denominations. These usually included two or three Presbyterian denominations, four or five Lutheran traditions, five or six Baptist groups, five or six Methodist bodies, the Episcopal Church, and a half dozen other denominations. Nearly all these denominations traced their origins back to before 1900, and most represented a western European religious tradition. In a landmark book, Will Herberg pointed out that religious affiliation had replaced nationality as the core of personal identify by Americans.[2]

During the 1950s the promotion of denominational mergers moved ahead of new church development on the agendas of several Protestant traditions. The resulting vacuum was partially filled by newer denominations created during the twentieth century and by a growing number of entrepreneurial individuals who organized nondenominational or independent congregations.

On the one hand, the denominational mergers tended to erode the distinctive identity of congregations organized before 1970. The erosion of denominational loyalties and the declining importance of "brand names" in congregations strengthened competition among the churches for prospective future constituents.

On the other hand, the emergence of new, and in many cases, large and growing independent churches also enhanced that competition.

The Forty-Year Syndrome

Another change in the ecclesiastical context began to appear two or three decades after that boom in new church development following World War II. The shortage of resources produced a severe cutback in new church development between 1930 and 1945. The end of the war and the subsequent migration from rural America to the cities that had begun in the 1930s, combined with the suburbanization of the urban population, unleashed a new wave of interest in starting new congregations that matched the 1919–29 effort.

Unlike many of the relocations of the 1950s that were largely motivated by a desire "to follow our members," most of these new missions were organized around a central evangelistic goal. "Our purpose is to bring the good news of Jesus Christ to residents with no active church affiliation." More than a few were launched to "serve people from our religious tradition moving into these new residential areas," but these were a minority. The majority focused on reaching the unchurched nonbelievers. This goal of reaching and welcoming strangers was at the top of the agenda in allocating scarce resources, including the time and energy of the founding pastor.

A couple of decades later it began to become apparent that the price of success included an adjustment in priorities. The original goal was to focus time and energy on the unchurched. When these strangers became members and leaders, they did not expect to be neglected. They expected that the congregation would continue to be organized in response to their needs, wants, priorities, and preferences.

In the early years, the pastor spent 40 to 80 percent of the week relating to the unchurched. As they were transformed from "unchurched" to "prospects" to "members" to "leaders," the pastor had to allocate more and more time to the members and less time to reaching the unchurched. One alternative would have been to add a minister of evangelism to the staff to continue that original evangelistic emphasis, but the money to pay that salary was being used to construct a meeting place for this new congregation. If that new mission grew very rapidly, even more funds were needed for more staff to serve the growing number of members and to pay for building program after building program. When the congregation plateaued in size, mortgage payments came ahead of adding staff in the allocation of scarce financial resources.

The typical pattern was that somewhere between year fifteen and year forty in the history of these new churches, the evolution was complete. What had begun as a worshiping community organized to reach the unchurched had evolved into a church in which the top priority was "to take better care of our current membership and their children."

This change in the priorities of existing congregations created a demand to launch new missions designed to reach new generations and recent immigrants. That increased the competition for prospective future members.

The Call for Help

One consequence of the combination of this increased competition among the churches for prospective new members and that forty-year syndrome was a demand for help. The first, but now largely forgotten, response was the rebirth of comity.

One definition of *comity* was that it was a rational and cooperative effort to be good stewards and not overchurch a community. Another definition was that it represented a desire to control competition. Typically it called for denominational officials and/or pastors of existing congregations to come together to review proposals for new missions. A common criterion was that the site for a new mission should be at least 5,280 feet from the meeting place of an existing congregation. This review and control process was limited to proposals for new missions submitted by the cooperative denominations. It was impossible to control the plans of noncooperating religious bodies.

A common result was that the proposed site for a new mission by a cooperating denomination, while close to ideal in size, visibility, and location, was rejected because it was too close to the meeting place of an existing congregation. That often meant that the sponsor had to abandon what appeared to be an ideal site at an excellent location in favor of a less suitable site at a poorer location. That was one way to minimize competition. It was not uncommon, however, for a noncooperative religious body to come along and purchase that ideal site for its own new mission![3]

A second, and far more constructive, response to these pleas for help came in the form of what subsequently became known as the Church Growth Movement.[4]

The Church Growth Movement taught those willing to learn that the congregation that had plateaued in size or that was experiencing numerical decline could reach new constituents. The principles and practices that emerged out of this movement have been utilized by literally thousands of congregations to reach, attract, welcome, serve, and assimilate new generations.

A third and unprecedented response is the rapid proliferation of resources that have become available to pastors, congregational leaders, staff specialists, denominational leaders, and lay volunteers who are interested in improving the quality and relevance of their ministries (see chap. 17).

One consequence is that at least a few observers now contend that the most prominent line of demarcation separating Protestant congregations is not the denominational label or the nationality of the founders or the location of the meeting place or the date when that congregation was founded or the size of the paid staff. They contend that all congregations fall into one of two categories. The smaller consists of those willing to change, to be driven by a vision of a new tomorrow, and to utilize this plethora of resources. The larger includes those churches in which the planning

34

and decision making is driven by memories of the past and by a conviction that one size does fit all.

Another way to describe that line of demarcation is to note that one group of congregations is determined to shape their ministry by what worked in the twentieth century in America to reach and serve the generations born in the first half of that century. A second group is open to studying the lessons that have been learned in recent decades about how to do church in the opening years of a new millennium. It now appears that the first group of churches will be most effective in reaching and serving the generations born in the first half of the twentieth century, while that second and smaller group will be most effective in reaching and serving those generations born in the second half of the twentieth century.

Can one congregation do both? The answer is yes, but that requires a new chapter.

CHAPTER TWO

UNIFORMITY OR DIVERSITY?

When I came here five years ago, two-thirds of the adults were past sixty, and they were nearly unanimous that they wanted to continue with a traditional presentation type of worship service with nineteenth-century hymns and a robed chancel choir," recalled the thirty-seven-year-old pastor of a congregation that had been founded as a neighborhood church in 1921. "The previous year, worship attendance had averaged one hundred twenty in a room designed to seat three hundred people on solid oak pews. They also told me they expected, because of my age, that I should be able to attract a lot of the young families who have been moving into the big old houses in this neighborhood. When I suggested that we gradually move toward a less traditional worship format, including more contemporary Christian music, I was told that was what my predecessor had wanted, and that was the primary reason for his short tenure here."

"What did you do?" I asked.

"My first year I spent listening to people and attempting to earn their trust. I concentrated on my role as a loving shepherd of an aging flock," explained the pastor of this congregation that was now averaging slightly over four hundred at worship. "I also enlisted four influential allies. One was a grandmother who had three adult children, none of whom were active in any church. A second was a thirty-nine-year-old third-generation member here with super bloodlines who teaches music in the local high school and leads a small rock group on the side. The third was a young man who operates his own computer service business. The fourth was a young mother who was born and reared here by parents who had both been born and reared in this congregation.

"Instead of concentrating on changing the status quo, as my predecessor had attempted, we chose to begin with a change-by-addition strategy," continued this creative pastor. "About a year after my arrival, the board gave us permission to add a Saturday evening service as part of an effort to reach younger adults. While this was not the ideal compromise, we agreed to try it for three months during the summer as an experiment, after which it would be evaluated by the board. The traditional summer slump saw our Sunday morning attendance drop below one hundred in July and early August, but by mid-August we were averaging nearly one hundred and fifty in the fellowship hall at our nontraditional Saturday evening worship experience. At the August board meeting, one of the older members suggested we should merge the Saturday evening crowd into the Sunday morning service in order to fill those empty pews. Our high school teacher, who is the nephew of the man who made that suggestion, urged that if a merger was the appropriate course of action in order to create the feeling of one big family, we should merge the smaller Sunday morning group into the larger Saturday evening crowd. That ended that discussion!"

"What happened next?" I inquired.

"That fall we secured permission to revise the Sunday morning schedule. The old schedule had called for Sunday school at nine-thirty and worship at eleven o'clock. The new schedule called for a nontraditional worship experience with a band at nine o'clock concurrent with a full Sunday school, plus the traditional service at ten-thirty, also with a full Sunday school. We focused the debate on three issues. First, our Sunday school had outgrown the available space. Second, we needed a schedule that would give people a choice between worship followed by Sunday school or Sunday school followed by worship. That was part of a larger strategy to move toward becoming a high-commitment church in which we expected everyone to be in worship and also in a learning experience every week. Third, a growing number of older members now go out to lunch on Sunday, and they wanted to get out of church earlier. We focused the discussion on how to become a high-commitment church and on pleasing our older members rather than on whether or not to add another service.

"Three and a half years later that early Sunday morning service, which we hold in the fellowship hall, is our biggest crowd," boasted this happy pastor. "That room will accommodate a little under two hundred for worship, and we come close to filling it at least three out of four Sundays. The Saturday evening service has turned out to be a feeder for it. When we began that Saturday evening service, nearly all of those who came were young childless adults. Helping to pioneer that new service proved to be an attractive entry point for them. Three years later a growing number have a young child, and many have migrated to the early Sunday morning service. Close to twenty have decided to attend at ten-thirty, so that traditional service now is a little larger in attendance than when I first came. Both that service and the Saturday evening service run about one hundred thirty in attendance.

"We weren't surprised to see a fairly heavy turnover among the people in the Saturday evening crowd. Given their age and marital status, that was to be expected. What has surprised us is that the crowd is getting younger and the music is more contemporary. In only a couple of years the median age has dropped by about eighteen months, and we now have a lot of eighteen- and nineteen-year-olds.

One consequence is that some of the people who helped to pioneer that service have now switched to the early Sunday morning service because it is a tamer version of what the Saturday evening service has become.

"A year ago the nominating committee decided, without my saying a word, that five of the members of the board should come from among the regular attendees on Saturday evening, five from the early Sunday morning crowd, and five from those who worship in the traditional service. While I am one of the few who know this, close to half of our money comes from those attending the traditional service, but nearly two-thirds of our Sunday school teachers worship at the first hour. A year ago we got a full-time twenty-eight-year-old associate minister who now does most of the preaching on Saturday evening, and we divide that responsibility at the early service. I do the preaching about forty-five Sundays a year at the traditional service."

"What's your next step?" I asked.

"Two years ago we purchased an old dilapidated house next door and tore it down to expand our parking lot, but we're still short of parking. One of our success stories is that most of our people do come for two periods of time every Sunday morning now, and that means one parking space accommodates only one vehicle. We use the parking lot of the supermarket across the street, but that has been sold and will be replaced by apartments. Therefore, we have three choices. One is to grow smaller. A second is to purchase adjacent properties to expand our parking. The third, and the one we are considering, is to relocate and build modern facilities at a larger site."

Five Lessons

The first lesson is that success often brings unanticipated consequences.

The second, and far more important, is that frequently the best tactic for initiating change from within an existing and tradition-driven institution is to avoid fighting tradition and attempting to change the status quo. A more productive tactic may be to initiate change by addition rather than by subtraction.[1]

A third lesson is to create new entry points, new groups, new classes, new worship experiences, new opportunities to be engaged in volunteer ministries, and new roles for reaching and assimilating new people. Younger people in particular are more likely to respond affirmatively to invitations to pioneer the new rather than to come and help perpetuate the old. This pastor created two new congregations within a church with minimal disturbance of the status quo.

Fourth, unlike that pastor's predecessor, who had single-handedly challenged the status quo, this wise pastor chose not to enlist for the role of a volunteer martyr. Instead this young leader recognized the value of allies, and especially allies with ties to the local power structure. An alliance of five skilled and committed agents of planned change who focus on initiating change by addition frequently can be a majority.

A fifth lesson is that for many people seeking to be part of a worshiping community the most "comfortable" size is an average attendance in the 120-150 range. What formerly was an "extended family" type of church has been transformed into a congregation of three congregations with minimal disruption of the worshipers at that traditional service. If the focus had been to triple the size of that one worship service of five years earlier, and if that had been successful, many of the older longtime members would have felt like saying, "Our church has been taken over by a bunch of strangers who display no respect for our traditions."

Is Federalism a Useful Concept?

Finally, this pastor used a concept that in American political history is called federalism. How could thirteen British colonies, each with its own distinctive traditions and unique history, come together to form a nation? The first attempt was to create a federation of semi-autonomous units. When that did not turn out to be an acceptable system of governance, the Articles of Confederation were replaced by a remarkably enduring constitution. *The Federalist* is a book composed of a series of eighty-five letters written in 1787 and 1788 by Alexander Hamilton, James Madison, and John Jay to explain and defend the proposed Constitution. The Federalist papers provide a systematic theory of how unity can be attained while continuing to affirm diversity. Those letters also explain why and how federalism can be a means of encouraging experimentation and a broad range of approaches to problem solving. Contemporary examples include a variety of systems for financing governmental services, for organizing state governments, for providing tax-funded educational services, for conserving scarce resources, and for socializing newcomers into the local or regional culture.

Seventy-five years later, the Civil War was fought to demonstrate that the affirmation of diversity did not include the right of unilateral withdrawal.

Today federalism continues to be affirmed in a huge variety of institutions as a way to encourage innovation and experimentation.

This pastor utilized the concept of federalism to design and schedule three different worship services to reach and serve three different constituencies. Unity is reinforced by one name, one governing board, one budget, one staff, one treasury, one meeting place, and one belief system; but diversity is affirmed by choices in worship and learning experiences.

The larger the congregation and/or the greater the demographic diversity among the constituents and/or the greater the theological pluralism among the members and/or the longer the congregation has been in existence and/or the larger the number of pastors who have served that congregation during the past three decades, the more likely the dream of combining unity and diversity will be on the congregational agenda. Federalism is one avenue for moving toward turning that dream into reality.

Scheduling three or four or five or six or seven different worship services under the same roof every weekend is one application of federalism in congregational life. When reinforced by two or three pastors with different personalities and different gifts, federalism can be a productive strategy, for building a very large intergenerational congregation that displays a high level of demographic diversity.

In the nineteenth century and the first half of the twentieth century, regional diversity in the United States was affirmed and honored through federalism.

If the goal is to affirm an even higher degree of demographic diversity and to become a multicultural congregation, federalism also provides a useful conceptual framework. The beginning step in this process often requires the members of what is a predominantly white congregation, drawn largely from the upper half of the economic/educational ladder of American society, to take a difficult step. That is, to accept the fact that many outsiders perceive the church to be an exclusionary fellowship. In many cases the congregation meets in a large and intimidating building, which conveys the impression to outsiders, "This is not the place for me." Putting up a sign that proclaims "Visitors Welcome" does little to dilute that image. In most cases the worship services are conducted in English, which is clearly an exclusionary signal to those for whom English is not the first language.

If the members are genuinely committed to their church's

becoming a multicultural parish, the next step is to rethink a basic assumption. Well over 99 percent of all Protestant congregations in the United States operate on the basis that "We invite you to come to our place and worship God with us." By definition, that is an exclusionary assumption. Therefore, the second step in implementing a federalist strategy is to change that operational assumption. "We are prepared to come to you, to study God's Word with you, to hear your concerns, and to worship God with you either on neutral turf or on your turf."

An increasingly common and relatively simple expression of this form of ecclesiastical federalism is the regional church that draws its constituency from a ten- or fifteen- or twenty-mile radius. In the old days, when neighborhood congregations were the norm and most parishioners walked to church, it was not uncommon for the minister to urge the members, "Invite your neighbors to come to church with you next week."

Today, when many of the members are barely acquainted with their neighbors, when religion and politics are far below the weather, sports, children, and vacations on the list of acceptable topics of conversation, the members may be reluctant to urge their neighbors to travel five or ten or twenty miles to worship with a congregation composed of strangers.

Instead of inviting those distant residents, "Come to our place and worship here with us," these multisite congregations open a second meeting place five or ten miles from the "home base." Several have opened a third and a fourth center. Consistent with the concept of federalism, each place develops its own culture, its own personality, its own indigenous leadership, its own schedule, its own set of priorities, its own financial base, its own missional outreach thrust, and its own community image. But unity is maintained through one belief system, one name, one pastoral staff, one governing board for overall policy making, and a range of common efforts. These unifying common ventures may include the relationship with a sister church on another continent, a shared campground, a joint youth ministry, shared specialized ministries, a cooperative leadership training program, joint off-campus local ministries, and trips to the Holy Land.

The reference point when the question comes up about what should be a joint venture and what should be left to the leaders at each site is, "Would the comparable responsibility be placed with the federal government or with the states?"

The most exciting expression of ecclesiastical federalism is the multisite, multicultural, and multigenerational model. The most widespread use of this model is called "The Key Church Strategy" and was created by the Southern Baptist Convention.[3] During the 1990s the best model of this concept of "One Church, Many Congregations" emerged at First Baptist Church in Arlington, Texas.

What Are the Price Tags?

The crucial lesson to be learned from the application of federalism to expanding congregational inclusiveness is that it carries a price tag. That price tag is the sacrifice of the goal of uniformity. If a denomination is organized on the principle that places a premium on conformity among the regional judicatories and the affiliated congregation, that means diversity becomes an unattainable goal. The dream of the same system of governance for every congregation or universal standards for ordination of pastors or the use of the same hymnal by all congregations or the use of only one language in worship or universal definitions of membership is incompatible with the dream of encouraging demographic diversity.

A second price tag on implementing the principle of federalism in congregational life is represented by the conflict between the temptation to allow local traditions to drive the planning versus creating an environment that encourages creativity, innovation, a strong future orientation, and intentional change. This often means asking long-tenured members to devote their time and energy to staffing outreach ministries and enlisting recent new members to accept the responsibility of becoming policy makers.

Third, it often helps if the big local celebrations are not commemorations of the past (the fiftieth anniversary of the founding of this congregation), but rather events that lift up, affirm, and give visibility to the new.

CHAPTER THREE

WHAT WILL THEY WANT NEXT?

I must agree that we're now living in a consumer-driven society," conceded a lifelong church member now in her late thirties. "But I don't believe a church should design everything it does to be responsive to what people want. There's a difference between wants and needs. People today need to hear the gospel! They need to be brought to a saving relationship with Jesus Christ! They may want the church to be a free babysitter. They may want a church-sponsored soccer league for their children. They may want to be able to park near the front door of the church even if they overslept that morning. They may want video clips to illustrate the sermon. They may want the church to hire a full-time youth pastor to be a surrogate parent for their teenagers. They may want catered meals rather than volunteer to work in the church kitchen. They may want three or four worship services every weekend so they can fit church into their schedule at their convenience. They may want entertaining sermons in order to stay awake. However, I believe the time has come for every congregation to set its priorities on the basis of what God is calling it to do and to meet the needs of people. I believe we're spoiling a couple of generations of younger people. They may want to come to church on Sunday morning in shorts, sandals, and T-shirts, but I believe they need to dress up to show respect to the Lord when they come into his house. Maybe I sound old-fashioned, but I believe our call is to proclaim the gospel of Jesus Christ, not to simply cater to people's wants!"

This statement was delivered during the discussion period in a workshop that included nearly a hundred congregational leaders, both lay and clergy. When she finished, at least a dozen "Amens!" could be heard loud and clear.

Two Models

A reading of the first four books of the New Testament reveals that Jesus used two different models in speaking to people. This deeply committed Christian and active church member followed one of them.

In speaking to large crowds of people, Jesus usually concentrated on what he believed the people needed to hear. To use contemporary American language, he had an agenda and spoke from his agenda. He came with something to say, and he said it.

Frequently, however, in speaking on a one-to-one basis with individuals, Jesus used an entirely different model. He often initiated conversation by inquiring about the person's hurts, health, or wants. He established a relationship with that individual by beginning the conversation on the other person's agenda.

If everyone in that Sunday morning service is a deeply committed and fully devoted follower of Jesus Christ, it may be appropriate for the preacher to prepare a sermon designed to communicate what those believers need to hear.

If, however, a team of three full-time people have been sent out to plant a new mission, they may spend several weeks asking people two questions. First, do they currently have an active relationship with any church in this community? Second, if not, what would they like to see a new church offer that meets their personal and religious needs?

As they talk with people in checkout lines at the supermarket, in coffee shops, in door-to-door calling, at the high school football game, in bookstores, on the street, in the hospital waiting room, and in neighborhood gatherings, they are listening for both wants and needs (see chap. 4). Rarely will they hear people declaring that they are looking for a church in which the females sit on one side of the room during worship, while the males are seated on the other side. Rarely will they hear younger women hoping to find a church in which women cover their heads before entering for worship. Rarely will they find people who express a longing for a church that offers a sixty- to ninety-minute sermon every Sunday morning. Rarely will they hear people state that their preference is for a church that prohibits instrumental music and sings from the psalter. Rarely will they discover unchurched adults who explain that they are still seeking a church that depends on pew rents for its financial base. Rarely will they find people who complain that they have been unsuccessful in finding a church that still prohibits the pastor from driving a motor vehicle on the Sabbath.

One explanation for this emphasis on listening is that today's adults tend to bring an agenda of concerns that are not the same as their grandparents. A second reason is that the unchurched often have a different perspective from that of deeply committed Christians. A third reason is the need to build credibility with unchurched adults. They can earn credibility by listening and responding to people's hurts, problems, needs, wants, and concerns. Only after they have earned credibility can they expect to have a meaningful conversation with the atheist or agnostic about Jesus the Christ.

It also should be pointed out that it is not unusual today for that worshiping community to include not only apostles, disciples, and believers, but also skeptics, doubters, inquirers, atheists, agnostics, seekers, and nonbelievers married to believers. It also may include believers who are drifting toward skepticism. In preparing a relevant message for that collection of people, the preacher usually must address hurts, wants, frustrations, and doubts as well as needs.

If that congregation is composed solely of deeply committed believers, and if the only priorities on the congregational agenda are designed to take better care of the current membership, then this is a simple issue. The focus should be on transforming believers into disciples.

If, however, that congregation believes it is compelled by Matthew 28:19 to seek to evangelize among the nonbelievers, it really has only two choices. The easy one is to send money somewhere to hire people to do evangelism on behalf of that congregation. The second choice is to identify the hurts of the unchurched and seek to be responsive to those concerns.

From Luxuries to Necessities

Finally, an eschatological issue must be addressed. For those congregations in which the leaders are convinced that the Second Coming is but a few days away, the decision is simple: Focus on what people need to hear. Christ is Lord and Savior!

In many other congregations, however, the leaders are uncertain about that date. As a result, they may place a high priority on reaching and serving the next two or three or four generations. One example is the new house of worship that is designed and constructed, partly because of the requirements of the building code, to endure for at least a century.

This raises an interesting distinction. The evangelistic strategy to reach mature adults often includes a different set of components from those of the strategy used to reach younger generations.

One example, described in chapter 2, is the preference of

mature adults for a traditional presentation-type of worship service, while younger adults preferred a fast-paced, high-energy, and nontraditional worship experience. A second example is that the congregation focused on the religious needs of people in their seventies often will include a strong emphasis on the Resurrection. The congregation focused on families with very young children is more likely to place a greater emphasis on the birth and ministry of Jesus.

One facet of the generation-to-generation evolution is that what once were rarely discussed luxuries have become necessities. That wooden privy in the rear yard of the church was replaced by a small unisex indoor restroom. The replacement building included two rooms, one labeled men and the other labeled women. When that congregation relocated a few years ago, the new building was designed with two restrooms on each floor plus small ones between each of the classrooms in the children's wing.

The wooden sheds to shelter the horses in 1905 were razed in 1925 to provide a place to park automobiles. The gravel-surfaced parking lot of 1955 has been replaced by a paved lot three times that size.

Telephones, typewriters, air conditioners, copy machines, computers, a public address system, video projectors, and lighting controlled from the pulpit have become commonplace. The dated Sunday school materials have been replaced by customized resources. The advertisement in the local newspaper was replaced by television and, more recently, by a Web site on the Internet as the number-one channel for inviting people to church.

The old format of worship followed by Sunday school followed by a carbon copy of that earlier worship service is being replaced by four different worship services on Sunday morning with two concurrent services, followed by two other concurrent services and learning opportunities at both periods.

Instead of asking parents to take turns providing childcare during weekday or weeknight events, the church provides free childcare whenever parents are expected to be at church.

The old entry points for potential first-time visitors were largely on Sunday morning. Today that long list includes several Twelve-Step mutual support groups; a weekday nursery school; a coed volleyball league; after-school programming five days a week; Saturday evening worship; two and one half hour Monday evening, Thursday morning, and Saturday morning in-depth Bible study groups; prayer cells that meet in office buildings; a men's softball league; off-campus retreats; accepting responsibility for constructing or rehabilitating a Habitat for Humanity house; a ten-day trip to the Holy Land; and parenting classes. Today it is not unusual for a majority of recent new members to report that their first contact with that congregation came during the week, and not on Sunday morning.

Where will it all end? No one knows. The only safe prediction is that the thirty-five-year-olds of 2025 will bring a longer list of expectations to the church than did the thirty-five-year-olds of 1990.

That is one lesson. A second is, The younger the nonbeliever, the more likely that anyone seeking to confront that person with the good news of Jesus Christ, the more likely that an effective beginning point will be to initiate the relationships on the nonbeliever's agenda.

A third lesson is that the younger the first-time visitor, the more likely his or her decision about whether to return will be based on the choice of music, the relevance of the sermon, the communication skills of the messenger proclaiming the gospel, the age of the worshipers, the pace of that worship experience, and, frequently most influential of all, the question, "Are there other people here like me?"

Fourth, nearly every American resident born after World War I grew up in a culture in which electricity has become an accepted necessity. It is not a luxury!

The encyclopedia states that Thomas A. Edison died in 1931 at age eighty-two, but his legacy lives on. For most of Edison's life, church buildings had to be constructed with windows to admit light and for ventilation. Electric lights and electric-powered air conditioning are now commonplace. Therefore, it should not be surprising to discover that younger generations not only expect to find easily accessible, conveniently located, modern, and clean restrooms in church, but that they also expect comfortable temperatures and excellent lighting in all rooms in the building.

One consequence of Edison's legacy is the windowless room for worship. If it does have windows, they usually are at a high level and can be completely covered by a remote-controlled set of blinds. That makes it convenient to project visual images on screens. These may include announcements, a twelve-minute videotape, "The week in the life of this parish," shown before the beginning of each worship service, the words of every song or hymn to be sung, the words for unison prayers, an outline of the sermon as it is being delivered, interspersed with video clips to illustrate a particular point, and invitations to future events and programs.

An increasingly common design is to place the worship center as a two- or three-story room in or near the center of the building surrounded by a corridor with rooms, offices, perhaps a chapel, and the nave ("milling around place") on the other side of that corridor.

While he was not an architect, Thomas A. Edison has had a tremendous impact on the expectations younger generations, reared in a culture dominated by visual communication, bring with them to church!

Who Knows Best?

A persuasive argument can be made that the most significant change in the context for the parish ministry in the twentieth century is a product of the civil rights movement combined with the nationwide protest against U.S. involvement in the war in Vietnam.

These two protest movements undermined the credibility of "received wisdom" from older generations and from the respected institutions of American society. Most adults born before 1935 had been socialized into a culture that taught children and youth that parents know best. The public school systems in the United States had been created on the assumption that professional educators were better prepared than parents to make decisions about the education of their children. Colleges and universities were expected to fill the role of surrogate parents for students. The Great Depression encouraged voters to expect that the federal government knew best how to create full employment. World War II was organized on the assumption that generals knew best how to defeat the enemy. American-born black people were expected to agree that whites knew best when the role of African Americans was being defined. Women were permitted to organize missionary societies as long as the money the women raised was spent by men. Employers knew best about the appropriate working conditions and compensation for their employees.

One of the responsibilities of American-born white men was to teach recent immigrants their place. For a patient to challenge the diagnosis of a physician was one step this side of treason. If and when a parishioner disagreed with the pastor on a doctrinal statement or a point of biblical interpretation, that parishioner had two choices, "shape up or ship out." The owners of major league baseball teams knew best when it came to the salaries of the players. Roman Catholic and Methodist bishops brought far more wisdom and a better understanding of God's will than did either congregations or the clergy when the subject was the assignment of pastors. The role of stockholders in a for-profit corporation included cashing dividend checks, but it did not include challenging the executives or the board of directors. Publishers were in a better position to determine what books readers should purchase than were bookstore owners or book buyers. Social workers were in a better position than the needy to determine the appropriate assistance for the poor. The tenured faculty in the university knew best when it came to deciding on the working conditions and compensation of teaching assistants.

The first major and successful challenge to this old assumption that "they know best what is good for you" came with the efforts of organized labor in the 1930s. The emergence of militant unions in the automobile industry and in the coal mines introduced Americans to the concept of the power of the people.

The second half of the twentieth century brought the civil rights movement, community organizing, and the protests against American involvement in Vietnam. Martin Luther King, Jr., and Saul Alinsky introduced two different, but widely utilized, models for organizing protest movements.[1] These were followed by campaigns for women's rights, students' rights, consumer rights, employee rights, victims' rights, adoptees' rights, parents' rights, gender rights, stockholder rights, patient rights, and dozens of other liberation movements. Free agency became a right for professionals in major league sports. The Pentagon declared the United States cannot send military forces into combat without popular support for that decision.

Parishioners who disagreed with the pastor or with the policymakers in their denomination continued to exercise their right of withdrawal. Others, however, decided that, rather than leave, a better course of action would be to dismiss the pastor or replace those denominational policymakers. An even larger number decided to stay and ignore the pastor's point of view or to ignore the policy directives coming from denominational headquarters.

Respect for the authority lodged in the office of pastor or

bishop or mayor or governor or corporate chief executive or president or physician or professor or educator or general or editor or sports team owner or university president or high school principal or adult white male ain't what it used to be.

The American culture has been transformed as the consumers of goods and services and the people affected by new policies have become convinced that they know best what is good for them. Leaders without followers cease to be leaders!

How Do You Divide Up the World?

The protest movements of the past five decades have transformed American culture. These challenges to who knows best plus economic affluence have sparked the growth of consumerism. One consequence of consumerism is the abandonment of the old expectation that "one size fits all." One illustration of that is the multigenerational congregation that formerly scheduled two identical worship services for Sunday morning now offers people a choice from among four or five different worship experiences every weekend.

A more subtle change has emerged as congregational leaders began to design a ministry plan. When and how do we intervene in the lives of the unchurched as we seek to persuade them of the truth and relevance of the Christian gospel? How can we design our ministry so everyone will feel that we are responding to their needs? How can we make our congregation more inclusive?

Four Early Responses

For most of the nineteenth century the most clearly defined line of demarcation in ministry planning was gender. Women were welcome at the Wednesday evening prayer meeting, but, of course, they never spoke. Spoken public prayer clearly was man's work. In many congregations women sat on one side of the room during worship, and males sat on the other side. Men served as elders and deacons. Women worked in the kitchen. That emphasis on gender reflected the culture. Physicians were male, and nurses were female. Men made policy in the board rooms of office buildings during the day, and women cleaned those rooms at night. Pastors were male, and salespersons in the department stores were female. Men harvested the wheat and corn, and women provided them with hearty meals. Department heads were male, and women answered the telephone. The churches were in step with the culture as Sunday school classes were identified by gender. The Garden of Eden was proof that God wanted gender to be the key line of demarcation in classifying his creation.

In the early decades of the twentieth century in thousands of American Protestant congregations, this debate focused on language. The immigrant congregation worshiped in German or Swedish or Norwegian or Finnish or Italian or Spanish or some other western European language. Eventually the combination of births and deaths made this a divisive issue. One response was that the heretics who preferred to worship God in English left and founded a new English-language congregation. An alternative was to offer two worship services, one in the native tongue and one in English. A few tried to offer bilingual services, but that did not become popular until the 1980s. For most, the eventual solution was to become an English-language worshiping community or to dissolve.

During the middle third of the twentieth century, another response to diversity emerged in the teaching ministries. This called for the preparation and use of printed materials designed for a specific age cohort, consistent with the culture of that day.

In addition to gender, language, and age, a significant number of Protestant congregations used marital status in designing their ministry. Large congregations offered Sunday school classes for young single adults as well as for young married couples. In some churches, the twenty-five-year-old married man was eligible to be invited to become a deacon, but the forty-year-old bachelor was never asked. He could usher, but he could not become a policymaker.

In the 1960s, however, television began to undermine the concept of "age level" categories. Children and youth watched television programs designed for an adult audience, and adults enjoyed many of the children's programs on television.

The motion picture industry picked up the concept of using age as the system for classifying films and continues to use it, but it is widely resisted or ignored by many teenagers.

The last third of the twentieth century brought the emergence of several new systems.

Reaching the Unchurched

The Church Growth Movement generated the assumption that every Christian congregation should, by definition, place a high priority on reaching unchurched residences.

One widely publicized system focuses on the individual's personal religious quest. Various words and phrases have been used to identify these people, such as skeptic, inquirer, searcher, seeker, and pilgrim. One popular model of evangelism calls for a seeker-sensitive Sunday morning teaching experience for the general public and Wednesday evening worship services for believers.

This system sometimes is described as a faith journey approach. The worship, teaching, and youth ministries of the congregation are designed to reflect this system. Adult classes are designed for inquirers, for new believers, for believers who are self-identified learners, for learners who are ready to be challenged to become fully devoted followers of Jesus, and for disciples who are ready to be transformed into apostles.

The weekend worship schedule also may be defined by parallel stages of one's personal faith journey.

One common consequence is that the wife often is in a different study group and participates in a different worship experience from the ones chosen by her husband. Their sixteen-year-old son may choose a third worship service.

A more widely followed system focuses on the life cycle. This is based on the assumption that the unchurched will be most open and most likely to be responsive to the Christian gospel when they are experiencing a major change in their lives. These points include marriage, parenthood, divorce, death of a family member, retirement, a life-threatening illness, loss of a job, or some other crisis.

Examples are the mutual support group for the recently widowed, the weekend retreat for newly engaged couples, the new class for newlyweds and couples about to be married, a series of parenting classes for parents of teenagers, the weekly senior citizens' luncheon, the exercise class for those who want to look good at their open casket funeral, the divorce recovery group, the Sunday school class for parents in blended families, the class for couples in an intercultural marriage, the weekly evening class for new parents, and the mutual support group for younger adults who are still dealing with the divorce of their parents ten or fifteen years earlier.

Each one of these groups is designed as a short-term (three- to twelve-month) commitment to make it easier for the unchurched to feel welcome and to gain an early sense of belonging.

Gradually that focus on the life cycle can be expanded

and become the conceptual framework for designing the entire ministry plan and for developing the appropriate staff configuration. Age, gender, and language become minor considerations.

An extremely low-key approach to welcoming outsiders is based on the concept of affinity groups. These sixty couples rotate every month among fifteen groups of four couples each who enjoy dinner together at someone's home. These two dozen adults enjoy traveling together. One year they go to the Holy Land. The following year the trip is to follow in Paul's footsteps. The next year they go to Germany to study in Luther's path. They meet together every Sunday morning to reflect on the last trip, to prepare for the next journey, to look after one another, and to enjoy being together.

The central organizing principle of a third group is bowling. A fourth gather on Sunday morning during Sunday school to listen to and question an interesting speaker. A fifth group consists of quilters, most of whom are widowed. A sixth is a coed group, committed to helping others in need, who devote a day each week to what is broadly defined as volunteer community service.

Many congregations combine these systems to include one or two affinity groups, several classes or organizations or groups based on age or gender, mutual support groups reflecting the life cycle, and a couple of classes designed for people at different stages of their personal faith journey.

Recently a growing number of congregations have decided a high priority will be to strengthen the nuclear family. They have replaced the high school youth group with a package of ministries with families that include teenagers. The children's program has been replaced by a big package of ministries with families that include young children. These are supplemented by support systems for single-parent families and blended families.

What's the Problem?

It is difficult to criticize any of these approaches to ministry planning. Together they represent creative responses to the demographic diversity and theological pluralism of the American religious scene. Among the consequences, however, five stand out.

First, most agencies that provide resources for congregations continue to focus on age-graded materials. Two of the most highly visible examples are Christian education and youth ministries. There is a severe shortage of relevant and high-quality resources for other approaches to ministry. Teaching churches are beginning to fill this vacuum, but much remains to be done.

Second, the institutions preparing people for specialized staff roles tend to focus on functions (Christian education or worship or missions or music) or age. There is a national shortage of staff people equipped to help a congregation design its ministry around the life cycle or the family constellation.

Third, individual members of the younger generations tend to expect the ministry to be customized to their agenda. Some prefer a church with a ministry designed primarily around one's personal faith journey. Others look for the age-level design. Many are responding to the life cycle design.

This means that fewer than 4 percent of all Protestant congregations in the United States (those averaging more than five hundred at worship) have the resources, especially the people, to be able to fulfill the promise, "We are prepared to welcome and minister with everyone."

One consequence is the functioning obsolescence of the small neighborhood congregation. That was a relevant concept back when nearly everyone agreed, "One size does fit all!" Consumerism, however, includes a demand for customization.

A useful guiding generalization is that the greater the density of population, the higher the demand for customized responses to the consumer's agenda. In a sparsely populated rural area, one congregation may include one-half of the residents living within a mile of the meeting place. In the densely populated urban neighborhood, that proportion probably will be under 2 percent.

A few of the former neighborhood congregations have evolved into large regional churches. Frequently this has required relocation of the meeting place to a larger site. Most, however, have chosen either to carve out a distinctive niche or to grow older and smaller.

One related consequence is that the largest 4 percent of all Protestant congregations account for a larger proportion of churchgoers today than was the pattern in 1900 or 1950.

A fourth problem is that most Christian church buildings were designed to house worship, teaching, and staff. We do not even have agreement, much less an actual structure, for the design for a meeting place intended to accommodate a comprehensive package of ministries reflecting the life cycle of the average human being. The closest may be those rural and smalltown congregations meeting in a building with a baptismal font just inside the front entrance, a room for the corporate worship of God, a basement room for education and fellowship, and the cemetery just outside the back door.

Finally, it must be added that the designs for ministry based on language, gender, age, marital status, one's personal religious pilgrimage, the life cycle, affinity groups, and the family constellation cover only part of the ecclesiastical scene. The 1950s brought another design, one that calls for congregations to identify and offer relevant responses to the religious, personal, and family needs that potential constituents articulate as their priorities. Instead of beginning with what the church offers, this calls for beginning with the constituents' agendas.

The protest movement of the 1950s and 1960s caused the leaders in the mainline Protestant churches with a strong western European religious heritage to become aware of another approach to designing ministry plans. This created a debate that requires another chapter.

CHAPTER FOUR

SUBCULTURE OR NEEDS?

Our denomination-wide goal is to in-crease the proportion of our members who come from an ethnic minority heritage," explained a denominational official. "Last year our research department reported that Anglos account for 93 percent of our membership, Asians are 3 percent, Hispanics are 2 percent, and all others, including African Americans, are only 2 percent. We are placing a high priority on starting more African American churches."

"That's also one of our two top priorities in church planting," added a national staff member from another denomination. "Our goal is to launch seven new African American missions every year, along with ten new Hispanic congregations. The reason for the difference is that, thanks to our missionary work in Latin America since 1950, we have a larger supply of Hispanic church planters."

That conversation took place in 1995, shortly after "African American" had replaced "black" as the politically correct label for American-born black residents of the United States.

Another Perspective

"You have done a remarkable job here in building a very large regional congregation out of what began seven years ago as a new mission to reach African Americans." With those words I began the interview I had requested with the forty-nine-year-old woman who was the founding pastor of a congregation now averaging nearly seven hundred at worship. "I asked for an hour of your time so I could learn what you have done and how you did it. Perhaps a good beginning point would be for you to tell me a little about your personal pilgrimage."

"Neither of my parents ever finished high school," she began, "but both were determined I would graduate from college. For as long as I can remember, it was just assumed all four of us children would go to college. I went to the state university, earned my degree, and began teaching history in a large high school in the city. Every summer I went to graduate school, and I earned two master's degrees, one in American history and one in counseling. I did take two summers off to have a baby—one was born in late June, the second in early July three years later. After twelve years in the classroom, I was asked to apply for a newly created assistant principal position. The job description called for me to concentrate on reducing the dropout rate and on counseling students, but the principal made it clear he wanted help with discipline and with getting drugs out of the school."

"That's a challenging assignment!" I commented.

"Yes, it was, but it also was great preparation for what I'm doing now," she replied. "My husband and I were both very active in our church even before we married. In fact, that's where we met. When he moved here, he joined our choir, and our marriage was the third one to come out of that choir.

"About five years after I became an assistant principal," she continued, "I told my husband that I felt a call to the ministry. His reply was, `Do it!' When I said I felt I needed to go to seminary, he said, `Do it now.' That summer I enrolled in an eight-week summer school session at a seminary about ten miles from our home. I liked it, and to my delight, I found I had no difficulty keeping up academically. After three more summer sessions, I resigned as an assistant principal and went to seminary full-time for two years. During those two years, I also had a part-time job at a very large independent church as the number-three person in their youth ministries staff. I learned a lot there about how big churches operate, about youth ministries, and about preaching. In my second year, I preached at one or two of their six weekend worship services two or three weekends every month."

"How did your two children feel about their mother's decision to go into the ministry?" I asked.

"They were both proud as could be," she replied. "In a six-week period, we celebrated my forty-second birthday, our older boy's graduation from junior high, his fifteenth birthday, our younger son's birthday, his graduation from elementary school, and my graduation from seminary. We had a party every week for six weeks.

"Three months before I graduated, one of my seminary professors asked if I would be interested in planting a new African American church. I replied I would be, and he arranged an appointment for me with the denominational official responsible for new church development. He's white, and he came with a design I did not like, and it took awhile for us to come to an agreement. The compromise was that instead of my going out alone with the promise of a three-year financial subsidy, that subsidy would be for a maximum of fourteen months, and I could use those second- and third-year dollars for additional staff. I began work four days after I graduated from seminary with the goal of having our first public worship service in late August when school starts. It turned out that was an unrealistic goal."

At that point, I interrupted, "Tell me what you did in preparation for that eventual first service."

"The territory I was assigned is where we had been living for eleven years. It includes four suburban municipalities immediately east of the city. All four were developed in the 1920s for people who worked in the city but wanted a new house. About twelve years ago, as the whites began to move out, middle-class black families began to move in here. These four municipalities, which are one public school district, have a combined population today of approximately 50,000. About 40 percent are white, perhaps a third are African American, 20 percent are Latino, and the rest are Asians or immigrants from India. This is truly a multicultural community. I spent the first month or so going around talking to people, many of whom I already knew since we had been living out here longer than most of them had been here. To my dismay I found slightly more than zero interest in helping to start a new African American church. I quickly discovered there already were a half dozen flourishing black congregations in this school district plus several others that met in storefronts or homes."

"So what was your next step?" I asked.

"When I asked people to tell me what were their major concerns, over and over and over I heard the same three. The first was drugs. I was told a new crack house was opening every week. The second was youth. Most of the families who moved out here have powerful upwardly mobile ambitions for their children. They remind me of my parents, but they need help raising their kids. Since the high school I was in back in the city is black, I understood what they were saying. After all, my husband and I have raised two teenagers. Their third concern was the proliferation of gangs.

"So I revised my strategy. Instead of making my top priority organizing a new African American church, I decided my three top priorities would be to build a strong youth ministry; to work with municipal officials, the four police departments, the public school district, parents, and other churches to combat drug traffic; and, third, to help parents provide attractive alternatives to the gangs."

"That is truly a challenging agenda!" I exclaimed. "If I had been in your shoes, I would have begun by enlisting parents to organize a weekday preschool for three and four year olds and added one grade each year until we had a school that ran through grade five or six or seven or eight."

"That's needed, all right," agreed this wise pastor, "but in six years half of today's teenagers will be in jail or out on the street or dead. We need a preventive approach. This community needed a remedial strategy now! An old friend of mine who was a superb teacher in the high school I was in took the golden handshake and retired from teaching at age fifty-five. I asked him if he would join me and be our lay youth minister for a couple of years. He agreed, and he is still with us. We could only pay him $17,000 a year to start, but now we're able to pay the market rate. Next, I found a committed Christian at one of the city television stations to be our part-time media man. Four years later he moved to Denver and we replaced him with his assistant, who this fall started his senior year in high school. My husband agreed to be our volunteer choir director, and he still directs one of our five vocal choirs. My seminary helped me find a fifty-year-old woman who has specialized in adult education in general and in parenting classes in particular. She is European, but she is extremely competent, so her skin color is not a problem, and her age is an asset. She, my husband, my youth minister, and I have auxiliary roles here as surrogate parents and surrogate grandparents. Finally, I persuaded one of my seminary professors, a young white man, to give us two evenings plus Sunday morning every week for three months. By late July, that was my staff. When school started in late August, we recruited volunteers to help us deliver door-to-door on Thursday evening and Saturday morning 15,000 brochures. It turned out that the four of us on the staff plus our spouses, our children, and two dozen seminary students ended up delivering most of those brochures."

"What was in the brochure?" I asked.

"The brochure had five brief paragraphs. Each began with a question in big type. Do you want to help your teenager survive high school? Do you want to help pioneer a new high school youth group? Do you want to help pioneer a new church choir? Do you want to know more about what the Bible teaches? Do you want to learn how to be a better parent? At the bottom of the sheet, we explained that each requires a four-week commitment and that you could choose either Tuesday or Thursday evening from seven to nine. We had leased for a year what had been three vacant stores in a thirty-five-year-old strip shopping center, and all classes would be held there. The first week we had about sixty people on Tuesday evening and nearly eighty on Thursday. I led the group on helping your teenager survive high school. The seminary professor taught both Bible classes. My husband began to organize two new vocal choirs, one to rehearse on Tuesday evening and one on Thursday evening. Our specialist in adult education taught both parenting classes, and our retired high school teacher began to organize two new youth groups. The fourth week our combined attendance for all classes for both evenings was nearly three hundred. Each week we announced that the first public worship service for our new congregation would be on the first Sunday in October in our temporary meeting place. That fourth week we gave everyone a half dozen brochures to pass out to friends, neighbors, and relatives, inviting them to help pioneer this new church."

"I notice you make repeated use of that word *pioneer*" I commented. "Why?"

"First of all, we are convinced most people would prefer to help pioneer the new rather than join the old. In the new, the doors are wide open to strangers. In the old, the doors often are at least half closed. I saw that in high school. A newcomer to the community who was a ninth grader had a far easier time meeting and making new friends than the newcomer who was a twelfth grader. Second, most of the adult black residents in this school district are, by definition, pioneers. They pioneered the movement of African Americans into this area. My husband and I were pioneers when we first moved out here," explained this former high school teacher.

"We used the first two of those four Sunday mornings in September to visit other churches in this school district. Each of the six of us worshiped with a different congregation. We spent Sunday afternoon sharing experiences and reflecting on what we had learned. Thus in two weeks we visited a dozen different churches. We spent the next two Sunday mornings worshiping in our shopping center facility. We invited both of the choirs, both of the Bible classes, both youth groups, both parenting classes, and both parents of teenagers groups to meet at nine-thirty and to worship at eleven o'clock. The two choirs, of course, spent their time rehearsing. We did not, however, advertise those services. At noon on that last Sunday in September, we had over two hundred allies committed to making that first Sunday in October a success."

"You began with a study period followed by worship?" I asked.

"No, that was only for those two Sundays in September," she replied. "From day one we were determined this would be a high-commitment church, so in October we began with worship at eight, followed by learning at nine-thirty, followed by worship at eleven. We made it clear we expected everyone to be in a class at nine-thirty. Their option was early worship followed by study or study followed by worship. Our seminary professor was so enthused he not only agreed to stay with us for a fourth month, he also signed up a colleague for two months. One taught an introduction to the Old Testament, and the other taught the Gospel of Luke during October and November. Our youth minister taught what turned out to be a huge high school class. Out of the adults who had been with us in August and September, we recruited all the teachers we needed for children's Sunday school plus four other adult classes. For those first two months we averaged 135 at the first service, which was an African American format built around gospel songs. We averaged over two hundred at the eleven o'clock service, which usually ran until about twelve-fifteen or twelve-thirty. At that one we relied on a multimedia format with contemporary Christian music. From day one close to half of the worshipers at that second service were younger white couples with children. Today we run about two hundred at that early gospel service and a combined total of nearly five hundred at the two concurrent late services. One is the multimedia experience, and the other is more traditional. One of our associate ministers and I share the preaching at that first service. I also preach on most Sundays at the multimedia service. Our other associate preaches at that more traditional eleven o'clock service. That means people have a choice of either two or three preachers on about fifty Sundays a year. Each of our two associates preaches at all three services once a year. As a multicultural church, we have to offer people choices. I have a different text, a different sermon, and a separate bulletin for each of my two. The first service is almost entirely African American. The multimedia experience is multicultural, including thirty to forty adults in intercultural marriages."

By this time I felt sufficiently comfortable to raise a personal question. I asked, "How do you identify yourself? As African American or as black?"

She laughed and said, "I noticed you used black and African American interchangeably. I do, too. As you may have noticed, the Census Bureau used two dozen categories, including black, African American, and Negro, in their census forms for 2000. Now, to answer your question, my husband identifies himself as a black man. Our two boys are African Americans. After teaching American history for twelve years, I am proud to call myself an American. When did your ancestors come to this country?"

"On the German side, they came in the 1850s, and on the Bohemian side, they came right after the Civil War," I replied.

"Most of my ancestors came at least a hundred, maybe two

hundred, years before yours arrived. Therefore, if, as a third generation German-Bohemian, you can call yourself an American, I guess I have a right to call myself an American."

"How do the people in this congregation identify themselves?" I inquired.

"No one here seems to make a big fuss over that," she explained. "I know in some congregations that is a big issue. I have a friend, for example, in Chicago who is the senior minister of a huge Afrocentric church. It is not a black church, and it is not an African American church; it is clearly an Afrocentric congregation. Several blocks away, also on Chicago's south side, I have a good friend who is the pastor of what is clearly a black church, but these are two distinctly separate constituencies. Our congregation now includes several Mexican Americans, a modest number of Latinos, scores of whites, a lot of blacks, and an equal number of African Americans, a few Korean Americans, and a couple of Japanese Americans. My offhand guess is that the last two groups are outnumbered here by a three to one ratio by self-identified Americans with an Asian ancestry. Those ethnic labels are not a big deal with us. The number-one point of commonality tying our people together is that we all want our children to succeed in life. That covers everyone, regardless of race or nationality, and includes several grandparents. Nearly all our people moved out here to have a better environment for their children. That's why we moved here eighteen years ago. Second, we are trying to help people become fully devoted followers of Jesus Christ. It offends some people when we put that second, and I realize it may offend you. I place it second because that was my agenda when I was sent here, but I soon realized that agenda would produce a small congregation. To reach a larger number of people, especially unchurched adults and youth, we had to begin with their agenda first. They weren't about to listen to our message until after we had earned their trust by listening to them and affirming that their needs were legitimate

71

concerns that deserved our attention. As I told you a few minutes ago, I soon discovered their agenda consisted of three points, youth, drugs, and gangs. A third unifying thread, which overlaps the first two, is our widely shared goal of transmitting to younger generations a Christian value system and a Christian standard of ethical behavior."

"What you're telling me is you were asked to organize a new African American congregation, and you discarded that in favor of an agenda that the people you wanted to reach told you was their number-one concern. Is that correct?"

"You've got it!" she agreed. "Instead of an African American church, we now have a multicultural congregation, and I don't apologize to anyone for that. Let me jump ahead for a moment. We now have two full-time associate ministers. One, who is an excellent preacher, is a fourth-generation American-born male of mixed European ancestry and married to a lovely woman born in Mexico. He preaches at one of our concurrent services at eleven o'clock. The other is a black male married to a woman born in America of third- or fourth-generation Japanese American parents. You probably have noticed by my skin color that I have European ancestry, but I don't know those details and I don't worry about it. My husband claims all of his early ancestors were born in Africa, but I guess at least a fourth of mine came from western Europe. As I told you earlier, I call myself an American, and my guess is well over half of the adults here also identify themselves as American. The important point, however, is that most of us don't think in those terms. We're much more concerned about your progress in your faith journey than we are about your ancestry."

Separatist or Integrationist?

"The materials I have read about the Black Studies programs in various colleges and universities suggest they can be divided into two groups," I commented in introducing my next question. "The larger consists of those programs that are organized around a black-nationalist interpretation of American history. A much smaller number represent an integrationist ideology. If you are comfortable with that distinction, which of these two ideological positions drives your planning? Are you a self-identified separatist or an integrationist?"

"That's the easiest question I have been asked this month," was the instant reply. "But before we chase that rabbit, let me raise another issue. I agree with you that the interventionist versus black-nationalist or separatist distinction is important, but it is not the number-one dividing line within the black community. One of the things I learned while teaching in the city is the height of that wall between the immigrant black adult from Africa or the Caribbean and the third- or fourth-generation American-born black adult. If you study American history, you will see the conflict between the immigrant and the native-born has come up repeatedly. It is even in the United States Constitution. An American-born black can serve as President of the United States, but the African-born black cannot. I have a friend who was born and reared in Jamaica. She came to the United States to go to college. While in college, she experienced a call to the Christian ministry. She worked part-time to put herself through seminary. After she graduated, she went out to serve a congregation composed of American-born blacks. Her skin color is black. All of her ancestors came from an African lineage. After two years, she resigned. While serving that congregation, she became an American citizen, but she says she always was treated as an immigrant, not as a fellow African American.

"Now, to get back to your question. Originally I was asked by some white leaders in what is a predominantly white denomination to organize an African American congregation in this old suburban section of the metropolitan area. I accepted the assignment with the clear understanding that I would be completely free to develop my own ministry plan. After a couple of months of talking with both black and white residents, I quickly discovered most of them are integrationists. We had a lot of black nationalists among the teachers and the community leaders in that inner-city high school where I spent seventeen years of my life, so I believe I know the difference. Back in my old school, I would guess that today well over half of the boys and close to half of the teenage girls are separatists. If you polled all the black adults who live in this school district, I expect that at least four out of five would identify themselves as integrationists. If you polled the teenagers out here, that proportion probably would be a sixty-five to thirty-five division, with the majority being integrationists. You must remember that most of the black families who moved here knew they were moving to predominantly white neighborhoods. Their first goal was a better life for themselves and their children with a better school system as well as a safer neighborhood and better public accommodations such as supermarkets and retail stores. They didn't come out here with a goal of turning this into an all-black community! I'm sure most of those first black residents out here who thought about it would identify themselves as integrationists."

"What about the other churches out here?" I inquired.

"Most are monocultural," she declared. "We do have one large independent charismatic church that is a multicultural congregation. We also have about a dozen predominantly white congregations that have been able to attract a modest number of Latinos or a small number of blacks. There also is a new church with a pastor from a European ancestry who is married to a Korean woman that has attracted a couple of dozen other couples in intercultural marriages. About four years ago a young black minister who had majored in Black Studies as an undergraduate and subsequently graduated from a black nationalist seminary came out here to organize a black nationalist church. I don't believe his attendance ever got above sixty after the first month, and it folded after a year or so."

"Forgive my persistence," I apologized, "but how do you identify yourself?"

"You should have figured that out for yourself by now," she laughed. "Why do you think my husband and I chose to move out here many years ago? Of course, we're both integrationists."

"What do the denominational leaders who asked you to organize an African American congregation think about that?" I asked.

"First of all, I don't believe they had even thought of that distinction," replied this comfortable integrationist. "Second, and more important from their point of view, they're so happy with our numerical growth that they don't care that we also include a lot of folks who do not have an African ancestry. My hunch is they are happy that we don't need or receive any financial help, and they are delighted that we are in fact a multicultural congregation."

"We're about out of time, so here are my two last questions," I said in closing. "First, can you sum up in a few sentences what you see as lessons from your experience that could benefit others?"

What Are the Lessons?

"Let me summarize my experience with five statements," she replied. "First, it doesn't matter whether you are planting a new church or you are an old congregation trying to identify and reach a new constituency. Begin by identifying the pressing needs of the people you want to reach.

"Second, look for allies! I was asked to plant a new mission all by myself. Instead of doing that, I began by building my staff. After that, we, and that is a we, not an I, began an aggressive effort to enlist lay volunteers. That enabled us to begin our first Sunday with a guaranteed two hundred in attendance. We began as a large church that was staffed as a large church should be. My part-time job while in seminary taught me that a big church is not the same as a small congregation magnified twentyfold. From day one we acted like we were a big church. Those are keys to what you describe as our rapid numerical growth.

"Equally important, however, are the alliances we have made with a variety of other organizations concerned with the contemporary youth culture. They see us as a valuable ally. That list includes teachers and administrators in both of the high schools and in three of the four middle schools. It includes the police department, the mayor, and others in city government, and dozens of people from a variety of social service agencies. Our youth minister and I were among the seven people who took the initiative to organize a community youth council that services this entire school district. We knew the job was too big for us to tackle alone, so four years ago we took the initiative in creating a new alliance.

"Third, to pick up on a point you made, if you want to reach American-born suburban blacks, you should decide early in the game whether you want to reach integrationists, as we have done here, or separatists.

"As I told you earlier, I have a masters degree in American history. Therefore, I was interested to read about the organization of the new Historical Society. At their first meeting in 1999, they devoted one plenary session to the distinction you brought up earlier between black integrationists and black nationalists. A friend of mine who attended said this provoked a heated discussion and that some of the Afrocentrists became rather angry. The lesson here is that if you are part of a predominantly white denomination that wants to plant new missions to reach members of a minority ethnic group, you really have two choices. One is to focus on the subculture. For example, do you want to focus on Koreans or Korean Americans or the American-born adult children of Korean ancestry? Do you want to reach people who identify themselves as African Americans or those who identify themselves as black nationalists or those who are integrationists? Or do you want to create an Afrocentric congregation? Or a multicultural church?

"The alternative is to do as we did and focus on the needs and hurts of people, regardless of their ancestry, race, color, or ideology. By beginning with a comparatively large multicultural staff, we were able to define two points of intervention in the lives of people. One was the parents' concern for their children. The second, which we have expanded in recent years, is to reach people where they are on their own personal faith journey. That is one reason why we offer three different worship services on Sunday morning.

"Another reason we offer three different worship services is that upwardly mobile persons expect choices. This is as true among American-born blacks as among American-born whites. You may recall that about a year ago the ratings on television programs were published. They ranked the viewership of 144 TV shows. Seven of the ten that were most popular among blacks were the seven least popular among whites. People today are looking for a television program that reflects their experience and with which they feel comfortable. The same is true of worship. We are now planning to add a new worship service every other year until we offer seven different services. Forty years ago, when there were only three commercial television networks, a church could get by with offering only one or two worship services on the weekend.

"Fourth, one of the crucial decisions we made was to make real estate our fifth priority. Our first priority was to identify our potential constituency. Our second was to build a program staff. Our third priority, as I just told you, was to identify and enlist allies. The fourth was to enlist a big nucleus of people before we held our first public worship service. Now that we've built up a self-governing, self-expressing, self-propagating, and self-financing congregation, we are ready to move on to our fifth priority, which is a permanent meeting place. Next month, if all goes well, we expect to sign the purchase agreement to acquire title to this entire shopping center. We plan to divide it into two parcels. The west end will be owned by a profit-making corporation we have established that will rent out that space. Our church will have title to the east half, which will allow us to more than triple our current space.

"In five years we hope to purchase that west half and use it to house some of our new ministries, including a Christian school for young children.

"Finally, there is an old saying in show business that advises people to `Hustle what you have.' You said earlier that if you had been in my place, you would have started by creating a Christian day school for young children. That may be an excellent idea, but that would not be consistent with my education, my experience, and my skills. My skills are in working with teenagers and their parents. So that became our primary constituency when we began. The lesson is to build on strength, not on weakness."

"Last question," I declared. "I noticed that in your list of allies you mentioned several public agencies, but you did not describe any alliances with other churches. How come?"

"Most of the interchurch coalitions I have seen," she replied, "were built on a combination of weaknesses and wishes. We were looking for allies that could bring professional skills, experience, and other resources to these issues. That is a part of the advice I gave you a moment ago. Build on strength, not weakness!"

This pastor's advice opens the door to a subject that deserves a separate chapter.

CHAPTER FIVE

WHY TWO COMMANDMENTS?

Why don't the churches in this community get together to improve the life of the people living here? Most of them are too small to be able to have much of an impact unilaterally, but if they would cooperate, they could have a tremendous influence!"

This comment was addressed to the churches thousands, probably millions, of times during the second half of the twentieth century. One answer to the question was the growth of the ecumenical movement. Another was the huge impact the laity and the clergy had as they came together in support of the civil rights movement and against the war in Vietnam. A third was the growing recognition that the rhetoric from the pulpit was relatively ineffective unless it was part of a larger activist role.

Frequently cited parallels are (1) the ministers who preach on what the Bible states about becoming a more effective parent whose churches also offer a variety of ministries with families that include children and (2) the church that combines a heavy emphasis on teaching sermons with a variety of spiritual-growth opportunities.

Those and similar ministry designs have caused many of the laity to challenge, "I'm glad to see you preach against gambling, pornography, racism, corruption in public agencies, war, and other issues, but when will the churches around here come together and do something about those problems locally?" Sermons are useful, but alone they are inadequate.

The past four decades have produced a huge number of success stories as congregations have cooperated in a variety of community ministries. These include building housing for the elderly and for low-income families, feeding the hungry, visiting those in prison, providing support for pregnant teenage girls, offering job training for adults on public assistance, operating weekday child care centers, providing free medical and dental care for the poor, taking meals to shut-ins, operating clothes closets for the needy, staffing tutoring programs for public school students, organizing and operating Christian schools for the developmentally disabled and physically handicapped, teaching English as a second language, offering after-school programs for public school children, staffing parent-training classes for new parents, and dozens of other social services.

One criticism of these efforts is, "But why don't the churches do more?" Another is that in an effort to build a broad base of support from congregations of many different traditions, the proclamation of the good news in Jesus Christ is played down. The critics point out that as the years roll by, these ministries often lose their distinctive Christian identity and gradually begin to resemble the social-service programs operated by secular and governmental agencies.

Three Perspectives

Most of the comments about congregational involvement in community ministries can be divided among three categories. The most numerous, and the most uninformed, are illustrated by the opening paragraph. The churches should cooperate and do more!

A second approach calls for examining a sample of these cooperative ventures that no longer exist in their original form. What happened to them? Many disappeared after the individual who was the driving force in creating that cooperative ministry departed the scene. Others surrendered their distinctive Christian identity in order to secure funding from governmental sources, foundations, or corporations. At least a few failed primarily because of managerial incompetence. Others fell apart when that unifying cause, such as terminating racial discrimination or housing the poor or feeding the hungry, was replaced at the top of the coalition's agenda by a highly divisive issue, such as abortion on demand or American foreign policy or welfare reform or tax-financed school vouchers. For several cooperative ministries the key to their dissolution was the withdrawal of one congregation that had been providing a disproportionately large share of the leadership, volunteer workers, commitment to the cause, and money.

Another common, but far from universal, trend was that the original coalition was composed largely of congregations in which the initiating leaders were motivated by a combination of frustration and weakness. These leaders identified needs and issues that should be addressed by the churches, but their congregation was too small or had too few resources to respond unilaterally. The frustration level was raised when a majority of the members, often from a passive stance, placed institutional survival higher on their agenda than the challenge to address these unmet community needs. The hope was that the combination of unmet needs plus weakness plus weakness plus weakness could produce the resources required to respond cooperatively and effectively to these unmet needs.

Too often the result was a continued deterioration of the institutional strength of the cooperating congregations.

A third perspective comes from an examination of those congregations that have designed and implemented an extensive plan of community outreach ministries. What are the common characteristics of these success stories? From this observer's perspective, five lessons stand out.

Why Did They Succeed?

The most obvious common characteristic is that these tend to be very large congregations. In retrospect, this means they possessed the discretionary resources, either real or potential, that enabled them to unilaterally undertake and maintain their community outreach ministries.

Second, and this is in part a by-product of their size, they enjoyed the leadership of a long-tenured senior minister. He or she provided a necessary level of continuity in the definition of role, core values, priorities, relationships, trust, community image, and, perhaps most important, providing the appropriate training for volunteers.

Third, because this was the ministry of only one congregation, rather than an interdenominational or interfaith coalition, they were not inhibited in how they proclaimed the gospel of Jesus Christ. There was no need to water down that message in order to avoid offending a partner in the coalition. That community ministry continued to be a cause driven by the power of the gospel. It did not evolve into a social-service program driven by the need to enlist more allies or to secure more external funding.

While they often entered into long and valuable alliances with governmental departments or private social-service agencies or, occasionally, with foundations, those partnerships never challenged which version of the Christian gospel will be the foundation for that ministry.

Fourth, and most important, a common thread among these success stories is that they began by obeying the first of what Jesus identified as the two Great Commandments. The top priority was on strengthening that vertical relationship with God. That not only provided the resources to move beyond institutional survival, but also the emphasis on the spiritual growth of people made it easy to enlist replacements as members died or moved away. Most important, however, this emphasis on the first of the two

Great Commandments became the core of these specialized outreach ministries. That answered the question of both the volunteers and the recipients of these ministries, "Why are we doing this?"

This combination of understanding the "Why?" and building a strong spiritual and institutional base has made it relatively easy for these congregations to either (a) respond creatively, positively, and unilaterally to the second of these two commandments and/or (b) be highly selective in that effort to recruit allies and to enlist only those that bring skill, strength, experience, and other resources to helping the neighbor in need. These coalitions are organized on the principle of combining strength with strength to fulfill that second commandment.

That is the fifth of these five lessons. Strength is a far better foundation for outreach ministries than is weakness!

CHAPTER SIX
FROM LAW TO GRACE

The conventional wisdom declares that a major change in the American religious scene during the last four decades of the twentieth century was the growth of evangelicalism and the decline of liberal Protestantism.[1] That is true, but it does oversimplify a highly complex issue. If the traditional theological spectrum is used to conceptualize and describe the American religious scene, it is easy to explain the decline of fundamentalism at one end of that spectrum as well as the decline of liberalism at the other end. In political, social, economic, and theological terms, American society has moved toward the center. While the "religious right" has received tremendous publicity in recent years, that is largely a product of the perennial search for a scapegoat.

A more useful conceptual framework is the distinction between law and grace. For many decades the conventional wisdom associated the emphasis on the law with fundamentalism and grace with the folks on the more liberal half of that theological spectrum. During the past few decades, however, new generations have revised that pattern. The new leaders in the rapidly growing evangelical movement began to place a much greater emphasis on God's grace and less emphasis on legalisms. This change can be seen very clearly in American Catholicism as well as in evangelical Protestantism.

In theological terms, liberal Christianity continues to

place grace above law, but in several religious traditions legalisms have gained a new emphasis in polity. One widely discussed example concerned the role of women in the church. The Roman Catholic Church and the Christian Reformed Church were but two of many examples of religious traditions that placed a greater emphasis on grace while concurrently relying on legalisms to perpetuate old traditions. On the liberal Protestant side of the ecclesiastical scene, the Presbyterian Church (U.S.A.), The United Methodist Church, and the Evangelical Lutheran Church in America continued to lift up God's grace while becoming increasingly legalistic in restrictions on pastors and congregational leaders.

So What?

One slice of this endless debate over law and grace continues among professors in theological schools, but the key lesson can be discovered from the behavior of the generations born after 1960 as they search for a new church home. The denominational label on the sign in front of the building has become less and less influential.

While it is a minor issue, one interesting example is the shrinking interest in church membership. "Joining the church" continues to be a relatively important agenda item in many of the religious traditions with a strong western European religious tradition. In several of the "made in America" Christian traditions, including thousands of the newer independent congregations, church membership is not an issue. Most of the newcomers have only one question: "Is this congregation prepared to offer a meaningful response to my religious and personal needs and to those of my family?" The question, "What do I have to do to join your church?" rarely is raised.

The number of "joiners" in the adult population in the United States continues to decline. That pattern can be seen in lodges, political parties, bowling teams, veterans' organizations, and churches. Concurrently the number of Americans searching for a meaningful worship experience that will nurture their faith journey continues to increase. Instead of looking for a church that "stands for God's law," most of the churchgoers from these younger generations are seeking a church where the gospel of God's grace is proclaimed.

One of the fastest growing independent and theologically conservative Protestant congregations in the United States offers only two promises to its constituents: "We won't beat up on you, and we won't bore you!"

The critics of this trend argue that (1) this places an excessive emphasis on the immanence of God and largely ignores the transcendence of God, (2) increasingly sermons are designed to speak to the concerns the worshipers bring with them to church rather than to proclaim the Word of God, (3) the historic focus on Word and sacrament has been replaced by relevance and music, (4) Easter overshadows Good Friday, (5) an excessive emphasis is placed on one's personal religious experience that minimizes the promises of God, and (6) excitement is not an adequate substitute for obligation and institutional loyalty (see chap. 7).

Whether one approves or not, in the contemporary religious marketplace in America, the New Testament story of God's grace is attracting more church shoppers than is the Old Testament account of God's laws.

Those seeking an "ideal balance" between law and grace are more likely to find it in African American megachurches than in white churches.

The theological spectrum that placed fundamentalism at one end and liberalism at the other extreme was a useful conceptual framework for classifying congregations in the 1950s. By the end of the twentieth century, however, a more useful frame of reference places legalism and grace at opposite ends of that spectrum. One interesting part of that pattern is that while the national or world leaders in several religious traditions are becoming increasingly legalistic in their rules on practices (that list includes Roman Catholic, United Methodist, Lutheran Church-Missouri Synod, Southern Baptist, Evangelical Lutheran Church in America, and the Presbyterian Church [U.S.A.]), large numbers of younger evangelical parish pastors in those traditions are moving toward a greater emphasis on God's grace in their preaching and teaching.

While far from the most significant consequence of this contemporary distinction between law and grace, it can be a useful frame of reference in comparing congregational newsletters. This contrast is illustrated by the comment of an active churchgoer who moved from Oklahoma City to another state, where he soon became an active leader at Central Church.

"We still get the weekly newsletter from the church we belonged to back in Oklahoma City, and that is the first thing I read when that day's mail arrives. While I like to keep up with my old friends back in Oklahoma, that's not the main reason I look forward every week to reading it," explained the ex-Oklahoman. "What I enjoy about it is that every issue includes several wonderful stories about what is happening in the lives of the people in that congregation. It is not a traditional church paper; it really is a report on God's grace. The focus is not on schedules or financial reports or meetings or pleas for money, but rather about how God is at work in the lives of people in that congregation. It's a joy to read. While I try to read the newsletter from our new church on the day it arrives, I don't look forward to it! It is a chore to read. The focus is not on God's grace, but on the law. Every issue has at least a couple of items in it that seem to be designed to make us feel guilty. The last issue included a reprimand to the congregation about the poor attendance for the special program on missions a couple of weeks ago; a warning from the treasurer that if all the people who are behind on their pledges don't catch up, the church will have to borrow money to meet the payroll this summer; a plea for more teachers for the Vacation Bible School; and a couple of paragraphs from the pastor begging us to go out and recruit new members. This is a bad-news church paper, not a report on the good news of Jesus Christ."

When headquarters is driven by the law and congregations are organized to celebrate and give thanks for God's grace, can institutional alienation be far behind?

This represents one of the most significant developments in American Christianity during the last third of the twentieth century!

CHAPTER SEVEN

FROM OBLIGATION TO ADVENTURE AND EXCITEMENT

What will be the most divisive issue in American public education in 2015? Will it be over increasing the financial support of tax-supported public schools and universities? Or agreeing on criteria and tools for the evaluation of these schools? Or raising the bar for anyone contemplating a career as a teacher? Or tax-funded school vouchers? Or the success of the experiments with charter schools? Or more tax-funded scholarships to offset rising college tuition? Or the impact of profit-driven private corporations on education? Or a shortage of adults who view teaching as a calling rather than as a job? Or a greater investment of tax dollars to construct new buildings? Or the failure of the public schools to educate "at risk" children from disadvantaged home environments? Or an increase in tax-supported boarding schools for both the gifted and the disadvantaged? Or the growing power of the teachers' unions? Or the failure of schools of education to prepare effective teachers?

It would be easy to extend that list for two more pages, but that is not the point. From this observer's perspective, the most divisive issue already is on the table. One side accepts the fact that by definition, as well as by historical precedent, for most human beings learning is a boring chore that must be accepted as an obligation to survive in our society. The physical, social, and pedagogical environments of most classrooms, from first grade through graduate school, are consistent with the assumption that learning is, by its very nature, a tedious task. The heavy dependence on a passive role for learners can be explained only by accepting the assumption that learning is an unexciting chore.

Advocates on the other side of this debate contend that learning can and should be a challenging, engaging, rewarding, high energy, active, and exciting adventure. They point to scattered examples of elementary school classes in physics or middle school classes in social studies or high school football teams or university classes in archaeology or on-line continuing education classes or the television program *Who Wants to Be a Millionaire?* or the preparations of the protestors in Seattle and Washington, D.C., in 2000 who became reasonably well trained in the art of protest or the interactive sites sponsored by museums on the World Wide Web or the transformation of museums from tourist stops into exciting learning environments or children's programming on public television.

The most highly visible example in American Protestantism is the transformation of vacation church school. In the 1950s it appeared to be an intensive version of Sunday school but with better refreshments. By the 1990s it had been reinvented to become an exciting adventure.

For at least 250 years after the first European colonists came to these shores, it was widely assumed that the road to a better life for young people was based on three requirements: hard work, a venturesome spirit, and persistence. Those were the themes of the Horatio Alger books for boys. Following the Civil War, a fourth requirement was added to that list: a good education. That led to a gradual increase in the number of public high schools.

"Going on to school" after completing six to eight years of common school evolved from a privilege for a fortunate few to an obligation. During the 1890–1950 era, state after state adopted legislation requiring children to attend school at least until their fourteenth birthday. Subsequently, compulsory school attendance until the sixteenth birthday became the legal norm. By 1970 high school graduation became the norm for most teenagers.

The possibility of twelve to sixteen more years of formal education originally was an opportunity reserved largely for two groups of people: teenagers born into well-to-do families and exceptionally ambitious youth. Over the next century that evolved from an opportunity into an obligation and eventually into a requirement. Volunteers are more likely than unwilling recruits to perceive learning as an adventure rather than as a chore.

In today's American culture the typical four-year-old boy is likely to perceive nursery school as an adventure one looks forward to with both eagerness and trepidation. A dozen years later that youngster may see the last two years of high school as the remainder of a boring sentence that stands between him and freedom.

In recent years the shortage of semi-skilled and especially of highly skilled workers has forced many employers to transform the environment of their workplace. What once was a repulsive, often noisy, dirty, and disruptive work environment has been transformed into an attractive place. Many have even gone so far as to make the workplace a more attractive environment than many of the homes in which the employees live.[1]

The old economic culture was represented by the mutual obligation of "a full day's work for a full day's pay." Those nine words summarized the obligations of both the employee and the employer.

To retain the commitment and services of the best employees today, the employer is more likely to fulfill the dream that work can be a challenging and rewarding adventure.

Perhaps the most remarkable example of how to make learning an inviting experience is the Weather Channel on cable television. When it began to broadcast in 1982, it was widely perceived as a bad idea. While viewers appeared to appreciate a forty-five- to ninety-second weather report on the evening news, who wanted twenty-four hours of it every day? Sixteen years after it was created, the answer was that an average of fifteen million viewers tuned it in every day. The operating profits for the Weather Channel climbed to $100 million annually by the year 1999.[2]

For many decades nine-year-olds perfected their skills in arithmetic by calculating the winning percentage of their favorite baseball team or the batting average of their favorite player. Youngsters delivering newspapers mastered the monetary system by making change when collecting from their customers.

Once upon a time it was assumed that a person had to be at least twelve or fourteen years old to be able to learn to type. Today five- and six-year-olds have mastered the operating system of a far more complicated machine called a personal computer.

Learning is far more difficult when it is a chore and far easier when it is an adventure!

The obvious parallel, of course, is the image received by the twenty-six-year-old church shopper. When asked, "Why did you pick this church?" a common response can be summarized in these words: "I grew up in a Christian family, and we went to church every Sunday. When I went away to the university, I dropped out of church. A couple of years ago, however, I realized I was missing something; so when I moved here, I decided to look for a new church home. The first four churches I visited were even more boring than the congregation in which I had grown up. A friend at work told me about this church. I came, and, to my surprise and delight, I found that worship here is really an exciting adventure."

That Dirty Word

Deep passions are aroused when the discussion moves to another level and someone introduces what is widely perceived as a dirty word. That word is entertainment. The university lecturer who is able to grab and hold the attention of three hundred undergraduates for fifty minutes often is dismissed by colleagues as "simply an entertainer."

Several years ago *The Lutheran* published a brief essay by Pastor Walter Kallestad in which he explained his concept of "Entertainment Evangelism." Kallestad relied on a dictionary definition of "to entertain," which calls for the host to be sensitive to the concerns and needs of guests. Any congregation that invites strangers to come worship with them should treat those visitors as guests and should be sensitive to their needs.

That essay evoked more hostile mail than the magazine had ever received in response to a single article!

One reviewer of Edmund Morris's biography of Ronald Reagan dismissed it as "show business."[3]

The critics contend that serious learning cannot be entertaining; it must be boring.[4]

Likewise, critics of many of the rapidly growing megachurches filled with the generations born after 1960 dismiss them as "entertainment centers, not real churches." Many of these critics are confident that the only vocal music that is pleasing to God will, by definition, be difficult for most worshipers to sing. The songs that praise God and his goodness and evoke feelings of joy and thanksgiving among the worshipers simply cannot be pleasing to God.

Likewise, the teaching message that grabs and holds the attention of at least seven out of eight worshipers for thirty-five minutes while explaining a difficult doctrine of the Christian faith cannot be as pleasing to God as the twenty-minute scholarly sermon that bores most of the worshipers for those twenty minutes.

What Happened?

Twelve- to eighteen-hour work days on the farm, sixty- to eighty-hour work weeks in dark, dirty, noisy, and dangerous factories combined with severe poverty, unpredictable weather, and relatively brief life spans taught most Americans that life was hard. The Great Depression of the 1930s, followed by World War II, reinforced the conviction that for human beings, like the birds of the air and the beasts of the field, life must be organized around survival goals.

Obligations were powerful forces that influenced the behavior of most Americans. Parents had obligations to their children. As the decades rolled by, those children were obligated to take care of their aging parents. Going to school, going to church, saving for one's retirement years, and paying one's bills were among the many obligations that gave direction to life.

World War II added another obligation. That was military service. From the presidency of Harry Truman through the tenure of George Bush, no one could be elected president of the United States without meeting at least six criteria: (1) thirty-five years of age or older, (2) born in the United States, (3) white, (4) Christian, (5) male, and (6) wartime military service. Today relatively few young adults reared in upper or upper-middle income homes feel an obligation to spend two to four years in military service.

The affluent American culture of the second half of the twentieth century taught younger generations that for them, like house cats and pet dogs, life was not simply about survival. It also included time for adventure, relaxation, meaningful relationships, eating for pleasure, pampering oneself, and fun.

The older generations, of course, knew better. Many lamented these changes in the American culture and explained, "What this country needs is another Great

Depression to teach these younger people what life is all about."

In retrospect, however, it has become clear that the number of volunteers eager to teach younger generations about the importance of obligations greatly exceeded the number of people wanting to reorganize their lives around obligations.

Five Consequences

One consequence is that most churches find it easier to use the power of obligation to enlist mature adults than to motivate younger generations to volunteer.

A second consequence is the increasing difficulty in designing a worship service that will be a meaningful experience for a diverse collection of churchgoers.

A third consequence is the conflict that is a product of a minister who organizes the world around obligations and a constituency that has been taught that all of life, including work, one's personal spiritual journey, vacations, and learning can and should be an exciting adventure.

A fourth consequence is the difficulty theological schools are experiencing in attracting younger entrepreneurial-type personalities who are convinced that the parish ministry can be an exciting adventure and who do not want to waste three or four years in seminary.

A fifth, and perhaps the most serious, consequence is the shortage of adults who are both eager and able to reorganize institutional expressions of the Christian faith that were created to articulate and perpetuate obligations into congregations and denominational systems designed to attract individuals to a challenging and exciting faith journey.

The deeply committed Christians who possess the gifts and skills to do that appear to be more interested in creating the new rather than in transforming the old.

CHAPTER EIGHT

IT IS A MORE COMPETITIVE WORLD!

The amount of money Americans spend on hardware and home supplies keeps going up every year, but the number of hardware stores continues to decline. Every year more people are admitted to the hospital, including outpatient treatments, than in the previous year; but the number of hospitals continues to shrink year after year. Every October the number of people worshiping with a Protestant congregation increases over the previous October, but every year at least 3,000 Protestant churches either dissolve or merge into another congregation.

These are but three of scores of examples of how American society is becoming more competitive. That long list of casualties also includes dairy farmers, travel agents, variety stores, and commercial banks. Competition produces casualties.

The parish pastor of 1950 was serving in a far less competitive environment than the parish pastors of fifty years later, despite the fact that the number of people worshiping with a Protestant congregation on the typical weekend in 2000 was at least 80 percent larger than in 1950. The number of worshipers has increased far more rapidly than the number of congregations, but the competition for constituents is greater than ever before.

Why?

The most obvious reason why is the gradual disappearance of the neighborhood church. The privately owned motor vehicle has made it easy for churchgoers to travel five, ten, fifteen, or twenty miles each way to church two or three times a week.

The congregation that drew most of its constituents from within a three-mile radius of the meeting place had only a few nearby competitors. The congregation that serves a constituency scattered over a seven-mile radius from the meeting place probably will be competing with five times as many congregations. ($3 \times 3 = 9$, while $7 \times 7 = 49$ in comparing those service areas.)

A second factor is the erosion of traditional denominational loyalties. The thirty-five-year-old of 1950 was far more likely to confine the search to one or two denominations when seeking a new church home than is the thirty-five-year-old of today.

Overlapping that is the rise of consumerism, described in chapter 1.[1] Instead of "hanging in there" when a divisive internal congregational disruption occurs, today's churchgoer finds it relatively easy to look for a new church home.

The erosion of denominational and congregational loyalties stands out repeatedly when new members are asked, "Why did you choose this church?" Frequently the response begins, "First, we were shopping for a new church home, and after visiting several other congregations. . . . "

This explanation introduces a third factor. In most communities experiencing a significant increase in population, that trend has produced two consequences. One is the planting of new missions. The second is the relocation of the meeting place of long-established churches. Typically both offer the church shopper (a) the challenge to help pioneer the new, (b) an invitation to be part of a worshiping community organized around a vision of a new tomorrow rather than memories of the past, (c) modern physical facilities including off-street parking, and (d) the message, "We need you to help make this happen."

Overlapping that is the fact that many of today's new

missions and relocated churches have grown into megachurches or, at least, very large congregations that can offer people quality and relevance plus an attractive array of choices in worship, learning, volunteer ministries, and fellowship.

It is not unusual today to go into a community in which the number of residents has at least doubled since 1950 and discover that eight of the ten largest Protestant congregations either were founded after 1965 or have relocated their meeting place since 1970 or are both relatively new and have relocated at least once or twice.

The new often provides formidable competition to the old.

In addition to being a more competitive environment for reaching newcomers, ecclesiastical migrants, and younger generations, six other points of competition stand out.

Where Are the Senior Pastors?

The least widely discussed, but perhaps the most serious, consequence of this higher level of competition is the national shortage of ministers who can serve effectively as the senior pastor of a very large congregation. Most of the effective senior pastors of large churches today fall into one of three categories. One consists of those ministers who bring the combination of high energy, passion, entrepreneurial gifts, an attractive personality, decisive leadership skills, and a high level of competence as a messenger of the gospel of Jesus Christ, plus the ability to earn the confidence of the laity by repeatedly urging what turns out to be the wise course of action. That is a large but shrinking group.

The smallest group includes those pastors who intuitively say the right thing at the right time, intuitively choose what turns out to be the right course of action, intuitively identify and enlist the right volunteers for the critical policymaking positions, intuitively select the right candidates to join that program staff, intuitively are able to predict with a remarkable degree of accuracy the probable consequences of every potential course of action, and intuitively know with exceptional clarity the exact role God is calling that congregation to fill in the months and years ahead.

A third small, but growing, group includes those pastors who carry a strong future orientation, who are remarkably comfortable with the role of team leader and conceptualize the staff as a team of teams with the majority of team members being lay volunteers; who are convinced that more wisdom can be found in five heads than in one; who are not threatened by the presence of exceptionally competent professionals on those teams; who are lifelong self-taught learners; who are comfortable putting their feet up and relaxing for a couple of hours while contemplating what God has in mind for this congregation to do next; who are exceptionally skilled in preparing and delivering teaching sermons that cause most of the worshipers to depart saying to themselves, "I'm sure glad I came today! That message answered several questions I did not even know how to ask"; who are convinced God is calling every congregation to transform believers into disciples and apostles; and who repeatedly explain, "My primary job is not to do ministry, but to make sure ministry happens."

As recently as the 1970s many theological seminaries that identified themselves as professional schools could enlist and equip candidates for that first group. It may be unrealistic to expect self-identified graduate schools of theology to enlist and equip candidates for that first group.

The candidates for the second and third groups are more likely to emerge from among the laity in the very large church, but most have difficulty comprehending the value of spending three or four years in a graduate school of theology as essential preparation. They are convinced that a more useful preparation would be to spend five to twelve years as an apprentice in one or two very large congregations.

One consequence of this competition for these gifted individuals, many of whom initially chose a secular vocation rather than the parish ministry, is a growing number of second-career ministers who are in their forties or older before becoming equipped to serve as senior pastors of very large congregations.

The most serious consequence, however, is that the number of Protestant congregations in America that average more than eight hundred at worship is less than half the number needed today.[2]

Where Are the Volunteers?

From the perspective of many parish pastors the number-one example of contemporary competition is the competition for people's time, energy, and commitment. The proportion of married women in the labor force nearly doubled from 17 percent in 1940 to 32 percent in 1960 and doubled again to 64 percent in 2000. (These figures overlook the number of farmers' wives who worked as unpaid help on the farm in the pre-1960 era.) Full-time homemakers often were the core of the volunteer labor force in churches during the first several decades of the twentieth century, but by 1980 that source of volunteers had shrunk drastically.

A second factor is the increasing number of adults who work at two jobs month after month and year after year.

A third factor is the increasing length of the journey to work. The church member who is home from work by five-thirty is likely to be more available than the member who doesn't get home until six-thirty or seven or who is out of town three or four days every week.

A fourth factor is the recent rapid increase in the number of one-parent families in which that parent has a full-time job.

A fifth factor is the increasing demand for younger parents to provide after-school and weekend transportation for their children to a variety of events, contests, games, and obligations.

A sixth factor in this competition for people's time is one that many readers will insist should be placed first. This is the powerful attraction of screens covered with moving images. One screen is on the television set. The other screen is on the personal computer.

While these changes have been partially offset by the quadrupling since 1970 in the number of retirees aged sixty and over who are not seeking paid employment, this trend has been most helpful to those congregations that specialize in ministries with mature adults.

Where Are the Teenagers?

Another perspective on the competition for people's time, energy, and commitment is illustrated by a statement from a staff member of a regional judicatory.

"We gave our daughter a good used car for her sixteenth birthday. She has a boyfriend whom my wife and I both believe to be a wonderful young man; she takes dance lessons for three hours after school every Monday and Wednesday; she has a fifteen-hour-a-week part-time job during the school year that pays her $11 an hour as an artist for a designer of web sites; and she is close to a straight-A student as a seventeen-year-old senior in high school. But she has only a very limited interest in church," commented the forty-six-year-old staff member of a regional judicatory. "She does go to church nearly every Sunday morning, but that is the extent of her involvement. Where did we go wrong?"

That paragraph illustrates the search for blame by tens of thousands of Christian parents who are deeply dismayed over their teenager's disinterest in church. A common response is for the parents to blame themselves. Another is to blame the teenager.

A more productive response begins with two questions. First, what happened? Second, why did that happen?

The answer to the first question is the competition for the attention, time, participation, and energy of teenagers is far more intense today than it was thirty or forty years ago. Affluence, television, peer pressure, a faster pace of life, the Internet, and the labor shortage are among the factors that have raised that level of competition. One result was that this particular teenager concluded that church was a low priority in the allocation of her time and energy.

Why did that happen? The most common answer is the congregation of which she and her family were members probably was offering 1975 models of a youth fellowship, a teenage music group, a high school Sunday school class, and opportunities for meaningful involvement to the babies born after 1985.

The church youth group of today is seeking the attention and participation of teenagers who live in a far more competitive culture than the environment in which their parents and grandparents were reared. For many of today's teenagers, choice has replaced obligation in their culture. Choice creates competition, and that often separates the winners from the losers!

Several American religious traditions aggressively encourage church members, and especially older teenagers, to serve a brief hitch as volunteers in a mission post on another continent. One component of the strategy to accomplish this is to ask every congregation to include in its annual denominational report the number of volunteers in overseas missions for the past year. What we ask to be reported elevates the level of importance parishioners attach to that allocation of resources.

Recently one denomination discovered that its congregations reported a combined total of more than 100,000 volunteers in mission for the previous year, but only 24,000 of them volunteered through the foreign missions board of that denomination. The competition to enlist volunteers in missions is far greater today than it was forty years ago! (See chap. 10.)

How Do You Reward Volunteers?

The competition for volunteers created by parachurch and other organizations in recent years cannot be overlooked. One example of such an organization is Bible Study Fellowship, which has enlisted tens of thousands of church members to participate in exceptionally well-organized study groups. Another is Habitat for Humanity, which challenges volunteers to be engaged in rewarding short-term projects. Far more numerous are the local organizations designed to minister with high school students or to house the homeless or to feed the hungry or to take meals to shut-ins or to operate a secondhand store or to help the disabled or to staff public park district programs or to volunteer in the local hospital or nursing home.

This competition has transformed the system for rewarding volunteers. Once upon a time volunteers were rewarded by fulfilling an obligation. Today the winners in this competition are more likely to reward their volunteers with the opportunity to meet and make new friends or to be enriched by a memorable experience or to master a new skill or to gain satisfaction from a job that is not only well done, but also provides tangible and visible evidence that "We really accomplished something worthwhile!"

Once upon a time the person responsible for enlisting and overseeing volunteers rewarded them with a polite, "Thank you!" The more thoughtful followed up with a brief handwritten note mailed to that volunteer.

Today's volunteer coordinator is more likely to elaborate on that word of thanks with the comment, "You really made a difference!" That oral reward is followed by a letter that also may include a color photograph, explaining in one hundred to two hundred words how that volunteer's effort really did make a difference.

Who Transmits Values?

Who will transmit to younger generations the moral values and the standards of ethical behavior that have been at the core of Western civilization for centuries? For nearly four centuries the Euro-American response was the nuclear family and the geographically defined Christian congregation. Subsequently that responsibility was expanded to include the tax-supported public schools.

By 1840 most of the public elementary schools represented an evangelical Christian religious culture. Evangelical Protestant ministers were greatly overrepresented in the leadership for public education. With rare exceptions no one challenged the responsibility of the public schools to inculcate in children a Christian moral value system and Christian standards of ethical behavior. Character building was a central reason for the existence of the public school system in America!

As a small but growing band of parents dissented, a second strategy emerged. This called for the creation of private Christian schools. That was an especially popular choice among immigrants from Europe, Roman Catholics, Congregationalists, Lutherans, and others. More recently, public policy has called for shifting a larger share of that responsibility from the schools back to the parents.

Currently that question evokes several responses. One calls for the public schools to teach character and transmit moral values. The United States Department of Education has granted more than $30 million to states to fund character education and values programs in the public schools.

A second strategy is to outsource that task to private,

nonsectarian organizations that do not reflect any specific religious heritage. A leading example is Character Counts! which is based in California.

A third contemporary response is to contract with a private organization that does not openly espouse a particular religious perspective, but does represent a clearly defined religious perspective. One example is The Curriculum Initiative, based on Jewish texts.

A fourth response is the recent increase in the number of Protestant congregations that operate a Christian day school. This is an increasingly common practice among African American and Afrocentric congregations as well as among white evangelical churches.

A fifth response is the organization of over two thousand tax-supported charter schools, many of which place a high value on transmitting traditional moral values and on character building.

A sixth response is the creation of new tax-supported military secondary schools.

A seventh, and rapidly growing, response is home schooling.

An eighth response can be seen in the increase in the enrollment in parenting classes.

A ninth is represented by demanding that criminal justice systems and social-service agencies provide a constructive and remedial learning environment for youngsters who have been apprehended for violating the law.

Who will define the moral values to be transmitted to children and youth born after 1990? A persuasive argument can be made that this is the arena in which the churches face their greatest competition today.

Where Are the Dollars?

For many congregations, and for those denominational systems that have depended on congregations to finance the denominational budgets, the number-one point of competition is for the discretionary charitable dollar.

Between 1950 and 2000, per capita personal income in the United States increased, in current dollars, from $1,501 in 1950 to $2,277 in 1960 to $10,037 in 1980 to $28,650 in 2000. That was approximately a thirteenfold increase between 1960 and 2000.

A more useful trend line takes into account the increase in the population. In 1960 the total personal income for all residents totaled $401 billion, increased to $2,258 billion in 1980, and to nearly $9,000 billion in 2000. That comes out to more than a twentyfold increase in current dollars.

Charitable giving by individuals climbed from $7.2 billion in 1960 to $40.7 billion in 1980 to $140 billion in 2000, nearly a twentyfold increase.

While exact statistics are not available, it is clear that the more slop in the hog trough, the larger the number of pigs scrambling for a place to eat out of that trough.

The most highly visible consequence is the increasing competition for the individual's charitable dollar coming from colleges, universities (especially tax-supported public universities), theological schools, parachurch organizations, retreat centers, hospitals, and a growing array of nonprofit institutions devoted to helping the poor, the handicapped, the oppressed, the refugee, the homeless, and the hungry.

The most significant consequence is the increased level of sophistication and competence in many of the organizations seeking to be the recipient of those charitable dollars coming from individuals.

The most subtle change is that while older generations were taught to contribute to institutions that would forward those dollars to another institution that would decide on their final destination, younger generations have been less willing to trust distant institutions. As a group, younger people prefer to contribute directly, or perhaps through their church, to an especially attractive cause. They appear to be less interested in sending money to institutions that will redistribute those dollars.

One evidence of this trend is the congregation that receives 50 to 70 percent of its annual receipts from its constituents to underwrite a unified budget that includes operating expenditures, mortgage payments, and a respectable amount for missions and denominational budgets. In addition, the members are challenged to contribute in the form of designated second-mile giving to specific needs and causes. That list may run from twenty to eighty items and range from extra support for the youth ministry to helping a sister church in Africa to subsidizing a weekday children's ministry to partial support of a missionary couple in South America to purchasing materials for a Habitat for Humanity house to expanding the parking lot to financing a new ministry on the Internet. It is not uncommon for one-half of the total dollar receipts to come from designated second-mile giving.

One of the clearest contemporary contrasts in motivating people to contribute money to the church is illustrated by the two different systems utilized by the two largest Protestant denominations in the United States. The United Methodist Church relies heavily, but not exclusively, on a system defined as "apportionments." Congregations and members have an obligation to support denominational budgets via these apportionments. The Southern Baptist Convention relies on the symbolism of two saints, Lottie Moon and Annie Armstrong, to motivate Baptists to contribute to two exciting causes, world missions and home missions. Which word is more likely to motivate potential contributors? Apportionments or missions? Which symbol is more likely to evoke a generous response? Headquarters or those two deceased saints, Lottie Moon and Annie Armstrong?

Finally, within several American religious traditions

there are two additional forms of competition for those charitable dollars. One is represented by an either/or question. Should congregations place a high priority on sending money to help finance the denominational budgets? Or should a higher priority be on building the ministries, constructing the physical facilities, and adding the staff required to reach, attract, serve, and assimilate younger generations?

A short-term perspective makes financing the denominational budget the top priority. A long-term view recognizes that the future of that denomination will be determined largely by the capability of member congregations to attract younger generations of churchgoers.

One compromise is for congregations to rely largely on the financial contributions their members make out of current income. The denominational agencies will rely largely on contributions from individuals out of their accumulated wealth rather than asking congregations to collect and forward those charitable dollars (see chap. 9).

That distinction between wealth and income emerged as one of the most important lessons for the churches during the last third of the twentieth century. Therefore, it deserves a separate chapter.

CHAPTER NINE
INCOME OR WEALTH?

What are the biggest differences between Yale and Harvard universities and the various national and regional judicatories (districts, synods, conferences, presbyteries, state conventions, dioceses, etc.) of various American Protestant denominations?

High on that list is Yale, which was founded in 1701 by clergy to train ministers and is exceptionally skilled in persuading potential benefactors to contribute large sums of money to that school. A five-year capital funds appeal, which was completed in 1997, set a new record for higher education with receipts of $1.7 billion (billion, not million!) dollars. That averaged out to approximately $800,000 a day for 365 days a year for five years.

That record, however, was soon broken. Harvard University, founded in 1636 to educate ministers, in 1994 launched a new university-wide fundraising drive. The goal was $2.1 billion. By the end of 1999 that effort had produced $2.3 billion, well over an average of a million dollars a day! A total of 172,000 contributors made donations.[1]

These are two examples of how huge sums of money are being raised to finance institutions of higher learning, both public and private. These also are two examples of the syndrome described as "them that has gits." Wealthy institutions, such as Harvard and Yale, are more likely to receive large gifts from individuals than are small institutions. Likewise, the Protestant congregation averaging 3,500 at worship is far more likely to have a full-time and highly competent staff member responsible for soliciting large financial gifts than is the congregation averaging 100 or 300 at worship.

The New Game in Town

The traditional approach to financing congregational and denominational ministries has been to ask people to contribute a portion of their current income to the church. The Christian standard is the tithe. Some Christians contribute more than a tenth of their income. Many more contribute less than a tenth. The gap between needed expenditures and actual dollar income frequently was and is filled by money-raising endeavors, such as dinners, bake sales, auctions, the contribution of agricultural products, rummage sales, bequests, income from investments, the sale of real estate, denominational subsidies, and contributions from non-members.

To understand the new game, which encourages people to contribute out of accumulated wealth, it is necessary to take a brief detour and look at the changing American economic scene. Today an unprecedented proportion of the 100 million American households possess substantial accumulated wealth. Some of this accumulated wealth is the product of frugality. The Great Depression taught a couple of generations how to save money, but many never learned how to be comfortable spending it.

Another chunk of this accumulated wealth has been inherited from frugal and prosperous parents. The biggest slice, however, is in assets that have appreciated greatly. These include land, stocks, family businesses, bonds, commercial real estate, stock options, and houses.

In statistical terms, one measurement of this change is that in 1980 American households owned about $1.1 trillion in stocks either directly or indirectly through mutual funds, pension accounts, and trusts. By 1999 that figure had increased tenfold to over $12 trillion.

The number of Americans with net assets of $1 million or more doubled from 2.5 million in 1978 to nearly 5 million in 1999.

For 1998 one million households filing federal income tax returns reported an income in excess of $450,000 for the year.

The wealthiest 2 percent of Americans who die each year leave a taxable estate valued at more than $700,000.

What is happening to this accumulated wealth?

Who Are the Recipients?

Currently huge amounts of money, much of it in appreciated assets, are being contributed by individuals and families to educational, charitable, and religious causes. Who receives those generous gifts?

One group of recipients consists of institutions of higher education. For the 1998-99 academic year, 1,034 colleges and universities reported a combined total of $17.2 billion in gifts—an average of $18.4 million per school. Twenty reported total gifts of $159 million or more. A dozen community colleges each reported total gifts of $3 million or more. The $20.4 billion total for all institutions of higher education was up nearly 11 percent over the previous year. That was the fourth consecutive year of double digit increases.[2]

Most of these large gifts are being received by institutions that display six characteristics. First, and this divides the players from the spectators, is the initiative required to go and ask families and individuals with substantial accumulated wealth to share their blessing. Those who refuse to play this game almost never win. The rare exception is when the supportive individual takes the initiative and delivers an unexpected gift.

Second, the winning teams have a skilled and persuasive

111

messenger who communicates the need. Third, typically that messenger focuses first on building a positive relationship with that potential donor.

Fourth, and some will place this first in importance, that institution has credibility with the potential contributor. Critics may dispute the validity of the basis for that credibility. In many cases most of that credibility is in the personality of the messenger and in the persuasiveness of the message, rather than in the institution or cause itself. In other words, aggressive players, whom others view as charlatans, are successfully soliciting large gifts in this big money game.

Fifth, that persuasive messenger represents an attractive cause as well as a credible institution and builds on that three-way relationship of donor, cause, and messenger.

Sixth, in today's world the winning teams usually offer the prospective donor a variety of attractive choices, and the donor can designate the final use of those dollars.

The Big Money Game

At this point the reader may interrupt with a vital question: Are those big contributions by families and individuals out of their accumulated wealth going to the most needy and worthy causes?

That question has two answers. First, sometimes yes and sometimes no. Second, that is not how this game is played. This big money game is being played under the rule that the recipients will be those who take the initiative to send a persuasive messenger to build a solid relationship with potential donors, who bring or create credibility, and who represent an attractive cause. A significant advantage is held by those who also can offer the potential donor a choice among several attractive causes.

This big money game currently is being played at three levels. The lowest or amateur level displays the least degree of effectiveness and produces the smallest dollar results. This game calls for the messenger to ask the potential donor to contribute to an institution that will forward the gift to another institution, which will decide on the ultimate recipients. One example is when a church member is asked to make a contribution out of accumulated wealth to that congregation, which will forward those dollars to a denominational agency, which will decide on the final allocation of those gifts.

The middle or minor league level is when the potential donor is asked to give to an institution that will decide on the allocation of the money. A common example is the congregation that asks constituents to contribute to a unified budget. The finance committee makes the decisions on the allocation of those dollars. The stronger the relationship between the donor and the congregation and/or the greater the credibility of the congregational leaders in the eyes of the constituent and/or the higher the quality of internal communication between the congregation and the constituent, the more likely this will produce an acceptable level of financial support.

The major league level calls for the persuasive messenger to offer the prospective donor a list of attractive and needy causes. The donor designates the ultimate destination of those dollars. One example is when a university offers donors a choice among endowing a chair for a professorship, helping to pay for construction of a new classroom building, expanding the library, providing named scholarships for needy students, renovating the athletic stadium, creating a new business school, or supporting other causes.

A congregational example is when a capital funds campaign includes paying off the mortgage, helping to plant a new mission, expanding the off-street parking lot, purchasing a video projector, and helping to construct a meeting place for a sister congregation on another continent.

A denominational campaign could include advance land acquisition for new church development, establishing a retreat center for spiritual formation, funding the first year of a congregation's ministry with college or university students, encouraging congregations to become multisite ministries, encouraging a congregation near a medical clinic to begin a hospice ministry, the resettlement of refugees, or helping to finance the construction of church buildings on another continent.

The most significant trend from a denominational perspective, however, is the shift in financing the annual budget of the regional judicatory. The traditional system has been to rely on a sense of obligation to ask (or coerce?) congregations to contribute to that annual denominational budget out of their receipts from member giving. Nearly all of that giving, however, comes out of the current income of the members. This usually produces one or both of two ceilings. One is a ceiling on the annual expenditures of that regional judicatory. The other is a ceiling on the ministry and outreach of congregations. It is not unusual, for example, for larger congregations to send an amount annually to denominational headquarters equal to the total compensation of one or two or three program staff members or a down payment on modernizing their physical facilities.

That means that many of those congregations fail to expand their ministry and outreach because of staff limitations. The staff are not hired because those dollars are being sent to denominational headquarters. The short-term goal is to fund the denominational budget. The long-term consequence is the equivalent of eating next year's seed corn. The financial base for that regional judicatory gradually erodes as congregations are unable to expand their ministries because of limited staff. The most subtle, and frequently the most insidious, long-term consequence of this system is that it teaches congregations that raising and sending money to other institutions is a higher priority than the transformation of lives or reaching new generations with the gospel or expanding the ministry of that congregation. The most subversive expression of this syndrome is when the amount of money sent to the denominational headquarters becomes the number-one criterion for evaluation of congregational performance.

The new game calls for financing a large share of the annual budget of that regional judicatory from direct gifts out of accumulated wealth, rather than from current income given to congregations. One pattern calls for the executive of the regional judicatory to create two circles. One consists of a group of members who have the capability to contribute at least $25,000 annually to the ministries of that regional judicatory. The executive meets with this group quarterly to explain what is being done, to celebrate victories, and to lift up unmet needs. The initial effort is to build relationships, to earn credibility, to communicate needs, and to create support groups.

A larger circle consists of members who could contribute at least $10,000 annually. The executive of that regional judicatory also meets with this group quarterly with a similar agenda.

A reasonable goal is that by the end of the third year the contributions from that first group will cover close to one-half of the annual budget of that regional judicatory, with another 15 to 30 percent to be supplied by that larger second group.

Who Is Playing?

This new game is organized around identifying and building relationships with individuals, families, and that rapidly growing number of family foundations that are giving accumulated wealth to charitable, educational, and religious institutions.

One indicator of who is interested in learning how to play this new game can be seen in the annual statistics on benevolent giving in the United States. In 1998 charitable

115

giving climbed to a new record high of $175 billion. That was an 11 percent increase over 1997. The gifts to institutions of higher education were up 15 percent. Bequests to all causes increased by 8 percent. Gifts to personal and family foundations were up 16 percent. Health organizations reported an increase of 20 percent. Contributions to religious organizations were up 5 percent over 1997.

Those who ask do receive!

It appears that the overwhelming majority of congregations and regional judicatories are unaware of this new game or feel incompetent to play it or choose to continue asking people to contribute out of current income. They find the dependency path powerfully attractive! Fred Smith has estimated that for the calendar year 1998 the 375,000 Christian congregations in the United States received $48 billion in contributions, nearly all from the current income of the contributors. While nearly all congregations and most regional denominational judicatories continue to depend on donors contributing largely out of their current income, parachurch organizations and a few hundred megachurches are seeking gifts out of both current income and accumulated wealth.[3]

Which do you expect will be in the healthiest financial condition in 2010? Those institutions that depend almost entirely on contributions from current income? Or those that seek contributions from both current income and accumulated wealth?

It is true that this is a free country. No one is forced to expand his or her thinking. It appears, however, that the strongest and most influential religious traditions in the year 2025 will fall into one of three categories. One group will consist of the high-expectation religious traditions in which nearly every constituent meets a series of high expectations, including regular participation in worship, progress in one's own personal spiritual journey, volunteering in doing ministry, tithing, and continuing study.

A second will be those religious traditions that, like Harvard, Yale, and other institutions of higher education, have decided to learn how to play this new big money game at the major league level.

The third group will be those who are able to motivate constituents to contribute out of both current income and accumulated wealth.

What Is Your Batting Average?

If the baseball analogy is used, institutions such as Harvard, Yale, and the University of Michigan are batting between .400 and .600.

This scale measures the quality of those six characteristics identified earlier—the initiative to ask, the persuasive messenger, the relationships, credibility, an attractive cause, and offering the donor the power to designate.

The overwhelming majority of Protestant congregations in the United States have a batting average of .000 because they are not playing. A few are batting between .050 and .200. A tiny number are batting between .300 and .400.

Perhaps 20 percent of all the regional judicatories in American Protestantism have decided to try to learn how to play this big money game, but most are either still amateurs or batting under .200.

A reasonable goal for the majority of regional judicatories is that by 2010 one-half of their budget would be financed by contributions out of accumulated wealth from individuals and family foundations, 15 to 25 percent from fees for services, perhaps 10 to 30 percent from income from investments, and the remainder from member congregations.

A reasonable guess is that one-third to one-half of all parachurch organizations are playing this game at the minor league level or higher and are batting between .200 and .350.

Several national denominational agencies are playing at

117

the major league level and are batting between .150 and .300 with a couple well over .500.

A Cloud in the Sky

From a denominational perspective, one threatening scenario consists of two components. First, congregations will continue to turn to teaching churches, parachurch agencies, independent publishing houses, retreat centers, entrepreneurial individuals, and profit-driven corporations as they seek customized resourcing for a new era in their ministry.

Concurrently, regional and national denominational agencies will expect congregations to fund their budgets. Sooner or later, a few of the congregational leaders will begin to ask, "If we pay outsiders for customized resources, what do we get for all those other dollars we send away?"

By contrast, those regional judicatories that concentrate on helping congregations to succeed already are reporting, "Never before have we found it so easy to fund our budget."

Four Lessons

1. This new big money game has arrived. For those who want to play, it offers tremendous opportunities for financing new ministries.

2. No one is forced to play this game. It is still permissible to depend on bake sales, pancake breakfasts, chicken dinners, and gifts from the current income of members to finance ministries.

3. To play the game at the major league level requires initiative and competence in those six areas described on pages 113-14. This means thinking outside the traditional box.

4. Institutions seeking to move to a higher level of performance usually need additional money to do that, and contributions from accumulated wealth can be a major source of those funds.

Chapter Ten
SEND MONEY OR PEOPLE?

What is the most significant characteristic that distinguishes one congregation from another under that broad umbrella we call American Christianity? In 1900 it probably was skin color in first place, followed by language and nationality. Tied for fourth and fifth place was the distinction between Roman Catholic or Protestant and social class.

What is that number-one line of demarcation today? The answer will reflect the value system of the person responding to the question. For those who include in the core purposes of a worshiping community the transformation of the lives of believers, a persuasive argument can be made around the response to the call to mission.

The traditional response for most of the twentieth century was to send money. A common example was the self-identified "mission-driven" congregation that allocated the first twenty or thirty or forty or fifty cents out of each dollar in the offering plate to "missions." In several mainline Protestant denominations the definition of missions included funds for the financial support of missionaries in other countries, planting new missions in the United States, social justice causes, subsidies for struggling congregations, campus ministries, supplemental salary support for low-paid pastors, pensions for retired ministers, subsidies for denominationally owned and operated camps and retreat centers, and the cost of staffing and operating regional and national denominational agencies.

In a few of the wealthier denominational families, that definition of missions also included sending money to church-related colleges and theological seminaries, ecumenical agencies, homes for the elderly, children's homes, hospitals, and other social-service agencies. That emphasis on sending money was consistent with the producer-driven orientation of the American culture for most of the twentieth century.

One simple and common example in the 1915–50 era was patriotism. Americans were expected to support, both personally and financially, the goals of the federal government. "Buy American" was a widely quoted slogan. Persons uniting with a Christian congregation were expected to take a vow of membership that they would be loyal to and support that congregation and that denominational system.

That also was an era when preaching was widely perceived to be the most effective means of proclaiming the gospel, of converting non-believers into believers, and of transforming the lives of believers. Formal education from first grade through graduation from college was organized primarily around learning via the spoken and printed word.

What Happened?

In 1943, for the first time in American history, the number of live births exceeded 3.1 million. Eleven years later that number exceeded 4 million for the first time. The number of deaths hovered around 1.5 million annually. As recently as the 1950s the American culture and its value system were largely controlled by adults born before 1930.

These people were reared in a culture that taught such virtues as patriotism, fulfilling externally generated obligations, obedience to authority, institutional loyalty, support for inherited traditions, and accepting the initiative of the producers of goods and services.

By 1975 those adults born before 1930 were being replaced by the generations born after World War II. By 1975 fewer than 30 percent of the adult population of 1930 was still alive. The United States has never had, and probably never will elect, a President born in the 1927–45 era.

By 2000 the number of adult American residents born in 1945 or later outnumbered those born before 1945 by a seven to three margin.

These new generations of adult Americans were reared in a different culture. Their parents and grandparents had been taught to read a book and write a report on what they had read. While in elementary school, these younger generations took an all-day field trip and were asked to write a report on what they had experienced. In the 1955 high school, a small number of boys experienced the thrill of playing football on Friday night while most of the boys and the girls watched the game. In 1999 well over 600 high school girls played on the varsity football team.

These younger generations have been socialized into a culture that has opened the doors to new experiences. The skateboard has replaced the bicycle. The IMAX motion picture theater brings a new experience to watching a motion picture. The college choir once spent a week singing in several churches in a two- or three-state area. Its successor takes a trip to Europe. The seminary student of 1965 took a week-long "plunge" in the inner city. The seminary student of 2000 spends a week or two or longer in Hong Kong or Korea or Latin America. In many congregations the traditional classroom format for confirmation has been replaced by a series of carefully designed experiences.

In the 1950s and 1960s the missionary on furlough visited churches and showed a series of color slides that illustrated the ministries on that mission field. In the 1970s and 1980s an increasing number of pastors spent a week or two touring a series of mission stations on another continent. Both of these efforts made it easier to raise money to support American missionaries in other parts of the world.

Today a rapidly growing number of American congregations create a "sister church" relationship with a congregation in another part of the world. Volunteers go and spend a week or two or three or more with that sister church. These volunteers serve as teachers, laborers on construction projects, models of a Christian parent, evangelists, pilots, nurses, physicians, preachers, sanitary engineers, and computer programmers. They work with both indigenous leaders and missionaries to help strengthen the witness of their sister church. They want to "go where the action is." As one volunteer who has served in Jamaica and Paraguay and twice in Africa explained, "To a large degree, the spiritual transformation of the volunteer is in direct proportion to the amount of hands-on experience working with nationals and the length of the tour of duty. The volunteer is not expecting the career missionary or the national pastor to be a tour guide, but rather a fellow disciple called to ministry. These volunteers know the nationals as fellow seekers of Christ, not as people who are blessed by the visit of an American for a week or two or three. For many volunteers, this is the first authentic experience of being used in service to God. This experience is undergirded before they leave as they are commissioned by their pastor as not only an ambassador from that sending congregation, but also as an ambassador of Christ himself. They leave knowing that they also are being supported by the prayers of the people in that sending church."

"The central reason we challenged these volunteers to go was to help strengthen and reinforce the ministry of our sister church," explained one pastor. "The big fringe benefit we did not anticipate is we sent fourteen volunteers. The folks who returned were not the same people we had sent. We sent Christian volunteers. We received back transformed and fully devoted followers of Jesus Christ."

How many churchgoers are able and willing to accept this challenge? Experience suggests that an attainable goal by the end of year three or four of this emphasis is between 5 and 20 percent of the average worship attendance.

What is the simplest and most effective way to transform comfortable believers into eager and impatient disciples? Challenge the people to spend a week or two or three engaged in doing ministry with Christians from a sister church in another country.

What is the simplest and most effective way to transform the complacent and low-commitment congregation into becoming a mission-driven and high-expectation church? Enlist 5 to 10 percent of the older youth and adults to accept this challenge.

What is the easiest and most effective way to increase the number of dollars contributed for missions? Abandon the checkbook approach, and replace it with the expectation that members and their friends should go and experience missionary outreach in another culture. That changes the context for raising money for missions from an obligation to an opportunity.

Experiences can be more powerful than preaching in the transformation of the lives of people on a faith journey!

CHAPTER ELEVEN

RENEW THE OLD OR CREATE THE NEW?

Why should this nation spend tens of millions of taxpayer dollars to organize and operate new charter schools when the American landscape already is dotted with 87,000 public schools?

Because it is easier, cheaper, quicker, and more effective to create the new rather than to reform the old.

Why do we have a growing number of success stories of new missions planted by rigorously trained teams and so few success stories about the renewal of long-established and numerically shrinking congregations?

Because it is easier to create the new than to renew the old.

In terms of capitalized value, why is Microsoft one of the largest corporations in the world?

Because IBM decided it would be easier and cheaper to renew the old rather than adopt the new, while Bill Gates concluded it would be easier, and more fun, to create the new.

Why does a regional judicatory decide to allocate 80 percent of its available resources to planting new missions in that large central city rather than to allocate those resources to the renewal of a dozen or more long-established and numerically shrinking congregations in that same central city?

Because (a) a dozen pastors are available who possess the gifts, skills, and experience required to lead the team that will plant a new mission in the central city, but only one or two pastors are available who bring the gifts, skills, and experience required to renew a dying church; and (b) it is easier, faster, and cheaper to create the new than to renew the old.

Why are the new denominations, movements, and congregations in American Protestantism attracting a growing proportion of younger churchgoers?

Because it is easier to create highly attractive new congregations than to renew the old.

Why is the number of women who are active and regular participants in the women's organization in that 110-year-old congregation shrinking year after year while two miles away a twelve-year-old congregation reports the number of participants in their women's ministries has doubled every two years for the past six years?

First, because the women's organization in that older congregation is attempting to enlist new generations of women in an organization that was popular and effective with women born before 1910, while that younger church has created a package of ministries in response to the needs and concerns of women born after 1960. Second, it is easier to enlist adults to help pioneer the new while it is far more difficult to recruit volunteers to help perpetuate the old.

The Homebuilders Sunday school class was organized in 1952 to reach and serve young parents. It peaked in size in 1967 with an average attendance of sixty-three. Three years earlier the Christian Endeavor class had been organized to reach and serve adults born during and after World War I. It peaked in size with an average attendance of sixty-eight in 1970. Today the Homebuilders class averages nine and the Christian Endeavor averages seven in attendance.

One plan is to recruit new members from among the newer people joining that congregation. Two members of the Homebuilders class are convinced that "if we could find an excellent teacher for each class, it would be easy to attract a dozen or more new members." The oldest member of the Christian Endeavor class is confident that "if our pastor would agree to come in and teach for six months, we would soon have a roomful of members."

A smaller and more reality-driven group urges a merger of the two classes. The possibility of a merger is supported by the Christian education committee, which needs an additional room for use on Sunday morning.

What Is the Issue?

What happened to create this divisive debate between renewing the old and creating the new? At least five components of the context help us to understand the deep emotional level of this debate.

The first component is political. The advocates of perpetuating the old usually outnumber those who favor creating the new. In only a few decades most of American agriculture has been transformed from a labor intensive way of life into a capital intensive operation. Those who want to perpetuate the small labor-intensive farm outnumber those who have accepted the arrival of the huge capital-intensive corporate farm. Politicians count the votes and year after year appropriate billions of dollars for agricultural subsidies. Ironically, a disproportionately large number of those dollars goes to the large corporate farm.

Likewise, several denominational systems are organized to grant voting rights to delegates from existing congregations, most of which were organized before 1930. There are no delegates in those policymaking forums to represent the members of congregations that could and should be launched next year.

Most policymaking bodies in American society are designed to overrepresent the past and to underrepresent the future. Therefore, proposals to perpetuate the past are likely to receive more support than suggestions to create a new tomorrow.

Protestant Christians in the United States in 1800 were encumbered by very few obligations to support religious institutions created by earlier generations. The nineteenth century and the first half of the twentieth century, however, saw the creation of a huge number of religious institutions. That list includes schools, hospitals, orphanages, homes for widows, theological seminaries, colleges, camps, retreat centers, denominational agencies, missionary societies, councils of churches, retirement villages, social-service agencies, children's homes, office buildings for a denominational headquarters, publishing houses, homes for retired missionaries, and counseling centers. By 1980 most denominations felt obligated to help finance institutions created decades earlier.

This introduces the second part of the context. A common statement among budget officers is, "It is extremely difficult to add something new to the budget. It is even more difficult to delete an item that has been in the budget for several years."

It was widely assumed that (a) most of these new institutions could not and should not be expected to become financially self-supporting and that (b) the most effective way to ensure that these institutions would continue to carry a denominational identity would be to provide them with a continuing annual financial subsidy.

These two assumptions guarantee a higher priority for subsidizing the old than for creating the new.

A third part of the context can be summarized in the word denial. A natural, normal, and predictable tendency of most human beings, and also of most institutions, is to deny that they are moving toward irrelevance or obsolescence. The fact that an institution no longer is fulfilling the purpose for which it was created does not become a reason to terminate its existence.

A fourth part of the context gradually surfaced during the past seven decades. For most of American history, financial subsidies evoked pity, shame, disrespect, and a variety of other negative responses. Self-reliance, sacrifice, and delayed gratification were among the hallmarks of respectability. As subsidies, both direct and indirect, evolved from a way to "help the poor and the helpless" into a benefit for middle- and upper-class Americans, they became respectable.

By 1970 financial subsidies had been transformed from a short-term response to the needs of the poor to a respectable entitlement for all income levels. The old question was, "How do we help the needy?" The new question is, "What's my share?"

This transformation has made it easier to subsidize the dying rather than to give birth to the new.

Finally, the older the person, or the older the institution, the greater the length of the past. When the length of the past is greater than the length of the time allowed for planning for the future, it is easy for memories of the past to outweigh a vision of a new tomorrow. In congregations this usually begins to become apparent somewhere between year fifteen and year forty of their history (see chap. 1).

This also becomes an argument for limiting the term of office of elected officials in government, business, and the churches.

Seven Lessons

1. While exceptions do exist, the general pattern is that congregations that have been meeting at the same address for more than forty years tend to give a higher priority to (a) perpetuating the past rather than to creating the new, (b) taking care of today's members rather than seeking to reach the unchurched, (c) maintaining the real estate rather than launching new ministries to reach new generations.

2. When a congregation's meeting place is destroyed by fire or a natural disaster, the natural, normal, and pre-

dictable response of most parishioners is, "How soon before we'll be able to rebuild on this site?" That represents the desire to re-create and perpetuate the old.

Frequently a more challenging and constructive question is to ask, "Does this mean God is giving us the opportunity to make a fresh start at a new site to reach the unchurched?"

The debate really is not over rebuilding here or relocation. The debate usually is between perpetuating the old and creating the new.

3. Seventy-five years ago a request for a continuing financial subsidy was enveloped in shame. Today the person who suggests terminating a long-term financial subsidy often is admonished by peers and by the recipients of that subsidy, "You should be ashamed of yourself for even suggesting that."

4. We have zero evidence that financial subsidies are a useful tool in strengthening the life and vitality of congregations, retreat centers, camps, theological schools, or other long-established institutions. Long ago farmers learned that subsidized cats catch very few mice.

The one big exception to that generalization in contemporary American society is that a persuasive case can be made for continuing public and private financial subsidies to thousands of cemeteries.

5. Institutions that are dependent on other institutions (in contrast to income from user fees, constituents, and individual benefactors) gradually tend to drift into an adversarial relationship with the institution(s) that provide that continuing financial subsidy.

6. A short-term (six months to two years) financial subsidy for a new mission is more likely to produce a healthy, self-propagating, self-governing, and self-supporting congregation than is a guaranteed financial subsidy over three to ten years.

7. The single best approach for any religious body seeking to reach, attract, serve, and assimilate younger genera-

tions and newcomers to the community is to launch three new missions annually for every one hundred congregations in that organization. A significant fringe benefit of this policy is that it usually will reduce the resources for continuing subsidies to institutions that will be healthier if they are forced to become financially self-supporting.

CHAPTER TWELVE

FROM 70 TO 52

The architect promised the building commit-
tee their new church would seat 350 in the nave plus forty in
the choir loft when this building was constructed back in
1967," complained the pastor of Grace Church. "This congregation has been declining in size for more than twenty
years. When I came two years ago, they were averaging a little under one hundred at the early service and not quite
twice that at the second service. Several of the leaders suggested we revise the schedule to have only one service on
Sunday morning to regain the feeling of one big family.
After two weeks, however, we had to go back to two services. The nave is comfortably full with two hundred, and you
really have to pack people in to accommodate 250. Why did
that architect deceive people by telling them it would seat
350 in this nave?"

"Don't blame the architect," I explained. "That probably
was a generous estimate back in 1967, but it was based on a
different population. The standards of 1960 stated a church
could seat seventy people for every one hundred running
feet of pews. If the combined length of all your pews here
in this nave adds up to five hundred feet, it was assumed in
1960 that it would accommodate 350 people at worship
plus those in the choir loft. That was based on seventeen
inches of pew space per person. Today the standard is
twenty-three inches. That means fifty-two worshipers per
one hundred feet of pews."

That is the current standard for seats in motion picture theaters, stadiums, and subway trains. People are taller and wider than they were in the 1960s. In 1960, for example, 43 percent of American adults were overweight. By 1999 that proportion had climbed to 57 percent. In addition, an affluent society has taught people to expect more space. That generalization applies to bathrooms, parking spaces, closets, classrooms, traffic lanes, kitchens, hospital rooms, the lobbies in public buildings, driveways, and libraries. The big exception is that the seats in coach class on most commercial airlines are still only seventeen or eighteen inches wide.

From 25 to 50

How many off-street parking spaces do we need?

The answer, of course, depends on local circumstances. The neighborhood congregation serving a constituency living within easy walking distance needs relatively few parking spaces, compared to a large regional church. The big city church served by an excellent public transit system needs far fewer than the suburban parish with a scattered constituency and no public transportation on Sunday.

A second variable consists of the local municipal land use controls. A common standard in the 1990s in many suburban communities was one off-street parking space for every four seats in the largest room in the building. That was easier to calculate if individual chairs were used to seat worshipers rather than pews.

The big variable, however, is, What year is it? In 1930, for example, relatively few churches owned a parking lot. In 1960 the rule of thumb was that twenty-five parking spaces, including street parking, were needed for every one hundred worshipers on Sunday morning. Forty years later it is not uncommon for the large and growing suburban congregation that is attracting large numbers of families with children at home, and averaging a combined attendance of six hundred at three worship services on Sunday morning, to report that three hundred parking spaces are adequate for forty-five or forty-six Sundays a year, but inadequate on Palm Sunday, Easter, Mother's Day, Christmas Eve, and one or two other occasions.

One part of the explanation for this change is affluence. It is not uncommon, for example, for the family that includes two parents, one seventeen-year-old, and two younger children to come to church in three vehicles. A second part of the explanation is the sharp increase in the number of one-person households from seven million in 1960 to eighteen million in 1980 to twenty-six million in 2000. A third part of the explanation is the restrictions on street parking. Municipal traffic engineers argue that streets were constructed to move traffic, not to store parked vehicles.

So what's the answer to that question? The simple answer is that twice as much off-street parking is needed today as was true in 1960. A useful rule of thumb is fifty parking spaces for every hundred people at worship on Sunday morning.

From 41% to 5%

"The top priority for every congregation should be to reach and serve the people who live within walking distance of that church!" declared a veteran denominational official. "Nearly everyone agrees that one of the goals of every city is to rebuild the neighborhoods. For most of American history, the healthy neighborhood was the crucial ingredient in building a healthy city. Our churches should be in the forefront of the movement to create healthy neighborhoods. That's the best single approach we can follow to reduce crime, to make it a better world for children, to provide safe schools, and to create an environment that encourages people to care for one another."

133

That call to re-create 1935 usually receives considerable intellectual and political support. The big barrier to re-creating the cohesive neighborhood of 1935 is that fewer and fewer Americans live where they sleep. One example of this is the growing number of Americans who live on a farm and commute ten to seventy miles each way to their job. People still neighbor with their neighbors, but now that often means their neighbors in the workplace, not their neighbor down the street or across the road from where they live. For many, the closest friendship ties are not with residents of their geographically defined neighborhood, but with fellow members of a worshiping community that draws people from a five- to twenty-mile radius of the meeting place. Their spiritual neighborhood has replaced their residential neighborhood as the source for friends in their social network.

In 1942 a Gallup poll reported that 41 percent of all employed Americans either walked or rode a bicycle to work. Only 36 percent drove to work, while 23 percent relied on public transportation. Fifty-six years later the Chilton Research Services reported that in 1998 only 5 percent of all employed Americans walked or rode a bicycle to work, 9 percent used public transportation, and six out of seven either drove their own vehicle or carpooled.

Four Lessons

These three sets of numbers document four lessons for those responsible for preparing ministry plans for congregations in twenty-first-century America.

1. A point of commonality far stronger than place of residence will be required if the goal is to re-create the neighborhood congregation of 1935. This may be place of birth, language, a common enemy, kinship ties, race, a long-tenured and extroverted pastor with a magnetic personality, an attractive and narrowly and precisely defined religious

belief system (the opposite of religious pluralism), a patronage-driven political party, or marital status. One of the more common examples of the new neighborhood church today is the congregation that meets in a building near the center of that new retirement village.

2. The younger the constituency and/or the larger the circle from which a congregation draws most of its regular worshipers and/or the more rapid the numerical growth rate and/or the higher the income level of the members and/or the larger the size of the congregation, the greater the need for a surplus of off-street parking.

3. The broader the bottoms, the more space that will be required to seat one hundred worshipers. In the North, add extra space for more clothing in winter weather.

In addition, since most people prefer to sit on the aisle, rather than in the middle of the row, it may be prudent, if cost is a factor, to add aisles and to minimize the number of rows designed to seat more than five or six worshipers. A common and economical course of action today is to use moveable chairs, rather than wooden pews that are permanently attached to the floor.

4. Since it is increasingly difficult for newcomers to meet and make new friends from among nearby residents, design your ministry to compensate for that fact of contemporary life. Add this question to the criteria used to evaluate every existing ministry and every proposed new program or revision of the schedule or expansion of the physical plant. How will this make it easier for people to meet and make new friends as they expand the size of their social network? The larger the size of the congregation and/or the larger the geographically defined circle that includes the constituency and/or the higher the turnover rate in the constituency, the more important is that question.

CHAPTER THIRTEEN

WHAT IS THE ROLE OF MUSIC?

For many soldiers and citizens, music was often the most effective and only medium to express their emotions. It provided an escape from boredom, hardships, and those moments of sheer terror that come with total war. It was not 'manly' for a soldier to whine, cry, or talk of how badly he wanted to go home—but he could and did sing about it."[1]

Music has been and continues to be an exceptionally powerful tool to create a sense of unity and to strengthen morale in military organizations. Music was a powerful motivational force in the civil rights movement of the 1960s. Music has been and is a powerful channel of protest in resisting oppression. Music was and continues to be the most powerful vehicle for creating a sense of unity on that first day of a great revival that fills an auditorium with a collection of strangers. The unifying power of music helps to explain why so many rapidly growing evangelical congregations devote most of the first fifteen minutes of that weekly worship experience to music and prayer. In 2000 the campaign managers for George W. Bush, John McCain, and Albert Gore recognized the power of music as the background for introducing various stages of their presentation at every campaign stop. In the fall of 1990, when the United States was preparing to wage war against Iraq in the Persian Gulf and space for the shipment of personnel, equipment, and supplies was at a premium, the United

States Army sent dozens of bands to the war zone. Music is a key element of the program when a high school or university football team plays against its most hated rival. For decades manufacturers have picked theme songs for introducing their products to potential consumers.

While ignorant grandfathers continue to demand, "When is that child going to begin to talk?" informed parents understand that the spoken word is no higher than fourth or fifth in the sequence babies follow in learning to communicate with adults. Touch, motion, and music come earlier.[2] Together they constitute the foundation, along with trust and curiosity, for mastering the spoken language.

The importance of music for expressing emotions that go beyond words is a standard component of weddings, funerals, reunions, and other occasions.

Another Perspective

In December 1999 the Union of American Hebrew Congregations, which represents 875 Reform synagogues, held its national assembly in Orlando. The president of the organization, Rabbi Eric Yoffie, delivered a sermon in which he pleaded for what he called a "revolution" in Jewish Reform worship. He urged that music be "participatory, warm and accessible." He referred to what he identified as the "new American style" of music in contrast to the traditional music that came out of the Jewish communities of eastern Europe.

The distinction that Rabbi Yoffie referred to can be duplicated in Protestant Christianity in the United States today. What are the clearest lines of demarcation that distinguish the congregations composed largely of adults born before 1950 and those composed largely of people born after 1960?

One common line of demarcation is how long that congregation has been worshiping in that meeting place. Those with the older constituency usually have been meeting at the same address for at least four decades. Those with the younger constituents tend to be congregations that have been worshiping at the same address for fewer than two decades.

An even more common line of demarcation, however, is music. The churches with the older members tend to choose hymns composed before the 1950s. Those with a younger constituency usually rely on what often is referred to as "contemporary Christian music."

The exceptions tend to be the long-established congregations with an aging membership that have reinvented themselves to reach younger generations by offering two or three or four different worship experiences every weekend.

The younger generations of Protestant worshipers in the United States tend to agree with Rabbi Yoffie. They prefer music that can be described as participatory, warm, accessible, or easy to sing and that evokes enthusiasm from the worshipers.

One result is that the choice of music for worship has become a divisive issue among both Christians and Jews in America.

Three Applications

"We plan to plant a new mission on the west side of town," announced a denominational staff person. "What should be our strategy to make this a success?"

First, identify as clearly and precisely as possible the people you expect to reach, attract, serve, and assimilate.

Second, accurately and precisely identify the religious and personal concerns that potential constituency expects the church to address.

Third, design your ministry plan to include addressing those concerns. A radically different design will be appropriate if the goal is to reach residents of that relatively new retirement community across the street from the proposed church site than if the goal is to reach unmarried and childless adults in their twenties.

Fourth, decide on the music that will be appropriate for implementation of that ministry plan.

Fifth, begin your search for a team of at least three adults who will bring the gifts, passion, skills, experience, theological perspective, and personality required to implement that ministry plan. (Too often a pastor is chosen before those first four steps have been taken.)

Sixth, work with that team in agreeing on the mileposts or criteria that will be used to evaluate progress in implementing that plan.

"We are planning on scheduling a Sunday evening worship service that will be for high school age youth and be largely owned, designed, and operated by high school students, plus four or five adults in a resource role. How do we begin?"

Again, the first step is to define which segment of the high school population you seek to reach and serve. Churchgoing children of members? Completely unchurched teenagers? That 8 to 15 percent of today's high school students who are deeply committed Christians? Students currently involved with a parachurch organization such as Young Life? The 5 to 10 percent of the student body who are widely accepted by students as "the kids who own this school"?

Second, carefully choose the music that your primary constituency identifies with and approves of.

"Next year we will be celebrating the golden anniversary of the founding of this congregation. Our current plans include a big weekend celebration, a special capital funds campaign to raise $50,000 for missions, inviting all the living former pastors and their spouses to return at our expense for that weekend, and preparation of a thirty-minute videotape that will recapture the highlights of those years. We plan to make copies available for purchase for $10 each so we can pay for a network-quality tape. What else should we do?"

One possibility is to find a musician who can write a hymn that will combine four qualities. First, it will be consistent with the theological stance of that particular congregation or religious tradition. Second, it will celebrate your fifty years of ministry and your faithfulness to the gospel. Third, it will be easy for people to sing. Finally, it will be suitable to be sung at festive occasions such as birthdays, anniversaries, and congregational meetings.

Fifteen Lessons

What have we learned about the place of music in the life of today's worshiping communities?

1. The larger the proportion of people who were born after 1970, the more important is music.

2. The greater the degree of anonymity among those present, the more important is music.

3. The larger the size of the crowd, the more important is music.

4. The larger the proportion of those present who are new here, the greater the importance of music.

5. The higher the value placed on active and enthusiastic

participation by all worshipers, the more important is music. (This helps to explain the importance of the soloist in presentation-type worship services and the limited role of the soloist in participatory worship experiences.)

6. The younger (under age six) or the older (over age sixty-five), the person the more important is music as a channel of communication as a means of expressing feelings.

7. The stronger the desire to project a clearly defined identity or self-image of that congregation, the more important is music. Music has moved ahead of denominational identity or geographical location as the "signature" for hundreds of new missions.

8. The shorter the tenure of pastors, the more important is music.

9. The higher the level of expectations projected of constituents seeking to become members, the more important is the role of music.

10. The higher the turnover rate among the constituents, the more important is music.

11. The larger the proportion of women or recent immigrants to the United States or persons who identify themselves with an ethnic heritage (Swedish American or Korean American or African American or Mexican American), the more important is music.

12. The stronger the attachment to the past, the more important is music.

13. The greater the emphasis in worship on the third Person of the Holy Trinity, the more important is music.

14. The faster the pace of the worship service, the more important is the role of music.

15. The longer the period of time devoted to a traditional ritual (baptisms, Holy Communion, weddings, funerals, reception of new members, etc.), the more important is music.

CHAPTER FOURTEEN

WHAT WILL THE WORLD WIDE WEB BRING?

When we moved to this retirement community back in 2006, we continued to worship every
Sunday morning with our home church in Iowa,"
explained a seventy-three-year-old woman in excellent
health. "Of course, we had to get an Arizona driver's
license, we are now legal residents of Arizona, and this is
where we vote. We didn't see any reason, however, to transfer our church membership. My husband and I both grew
up in that congregation in Iowa; we were married in that
church in 1962, and we raised all three of our children there.
Leaving that congregation was far more difficult than moving out of the same house we had lived in for nearly forty
years. Six years ago, in preparation for this move, I helped
to pioneer a weekly prayer group in our women's fellowship that meets over the Internet. When we began, there
were twelve of us, and nine lived in that community in
Iowa. One was a former member who had moved to
Vermont to be near her daughter after her husband died. A
second is a woman who is in the Army, had grown up in
our church, and is now stationed in Germany. A third
moved to Florida a few months before we started that
prayer group. One of the original members has dropped
out, two others have died, and one was widowed and
remarried and now lives in Seattle. The other woman who
was a key person in starting it decided late in life to go to
seminary and is now a pastor in western Iowa. I'm now liv-

ing here in Arizona, so that means only three out of the nine of us still live in the community where this prayer group started; but we still meet regularly every Tuesday morning for an hour or so over the Internet. The third weekend in July, we all try to get together for a couple of days back at our church in Iowa. Last July, eight out of the nine of us made it."

"Because of the time difference, in the winter the ten-thirty worship service back in Iowa is received here at nine-thirty, which suits us just fine," added the husband. "The pastor told us last July that during the winter they average about two hundred at that ten-thirty service in the church, but he estimates that somewhere between four hundred and five hundred are plugged into it via the Internet. He also told us that slightly under half of their dollar receipts come from the Internet audience and slightly over half from the resident congregation. He joked that given those figures, when he leaves the Internet congregation will have to be given a voice in the selection of his successor. The church can't afford a successor who is not acceptable to a majority of the worshipers. We've arranged a monthly charge against our credit card to pay our pledge."

"You may be wondering why we haven't joined a church here," commented the wife. "The answer is we have. We joined a local community church that doesn't worry about membership, so we're really members of two churches. They have church at ten o'clock, so we can't worship there, except on Christmas Eve and during Lent, but we need the sense of community and the chance to be involved in service. We are both regulars in a Thursday morning Bible study group, and I work in the pre-school program three afternoons a week. He is now chairing the Hunger Commission, which raised over $6,000 last year and gathered two tons of food to help alleviate hunger. Last January we went with a group of members the pastor led on a trip to the Holy Land. I've always dreamed of being on a boat on the Sea of Galilee, but I never thought it would ever be more than a dream."

"I also serve on the missions committee," explained the seventy-five-year-old husband. "Two years ago this congregation established a sister-church relationship with a congregation in Africa. Last winter we financed a trip for eight of their leaders to come here and visit us. This summer about twenty of us will go over there to help them build a church to house what is now a six-year-old congregation. We've already raised slightly over $100,000 to pay for the land and materials."

"One of the features of this new electronic world that we really cherish is the videotape our church back home runs before the beginning of that ten-thirty service," the wife pointed out with obvious delight. "That fifteen-minute videotape recaptures the highlights of the past week in the life of the congregation. Interspersed in it are thirty-second comments by a half dozen different individuals each week. One may tell about welcoming a new grandchild. Another may be a couple we have known for decades who describe a trip they just took. A third may be an old friend's recovery from surgery. A fourth may introduce a new member. A fifth may be a goodbye from someone moving away. A sixth may be a member telling about a new job. I sometimes think it's easier to stay in touch with the people in our church today than it was when we lived there."

"You could say we're having our cake and eating it, too," reflected the husband. "We can enjoy the warm weather in the winter without leaving the church that's been a central part of our lives for so long."

That imaginary conversation in the year 2011 introduces both the greatest unknown and the biggest societal change in the context for the parish ministry since the introduction of the privately owned motor vehicle began to undermine the concept of the neighborhood church.

The big unknown is that it will be 2020 or later before

anyone will be able to describe the impact of the Internet on how we do church in the twenty-first century.

One of the big changes was introduced earlier by television. Television enables people to be there without being there. Television has enabled people on another continent to have a better view of the departure of space vehicles into the sky or of football games or political conventions or protest marches or worship services or war or refugee camps or hurricanes than is available to those on the scene. Technological and financial barriers, however, prevented most congregations from televising their ministries to distant viewers until the early years of the new century.

Everything described in that earlier imaginary conversation was technologically possible in 1999, but will not be universally available until later.

What Will Be the Impact?

While it is far too early to begin to identify the most radical changes the World Wide Web will bring to congregational life, it is easy to identify a score that already are being experienced.

1. The automobile created the regional church, the successor to the neighborhood congregation. Television helped to create national constituencies for a few dozen congregations. The World Wide Web opens the door to the creation of international parishes.

For many churchgoers, moving out of town formerly meant shopping for a new church. The Internet makes it possible to move out of state and still worship with the same congregation.

2. The most difficult problem confronting 15 to 20 percent of all Protestant congregations in any given year is finding a successor for the departing pastor. The differences among congregations today are far greater than they were in 1955. Ditto the differences among pastors. How can a congrega-

145

tion identify a prospective future pastor who brings the gifts, skills, priorities, experience, personality, and theological stance that church needs at this point in its history?

One part of the answer is to turn from a regional to a national search for candidates. The second part is to use the Internet to build a list of candidates. The third part is to improve the system for describing that congregation. The classification system described in chapter 16 can be one part of that. A fourth is to use the Internet as a low-cost way to screen candidates.

3. The Internet already is being used to assemble a far larger crowd for Grandma's funeral service. The current technology not only makes it possible for distant or incapacitated relatives and friends to watch that televised memorial service, but it also enables a few nonresidents to participate with oral tributes to the deceased person.

4. Television raised the bar on what churchgoers believed they were entitled to in the quality of a worship experience or teaching ministry. The Internet will raise the standard another two or three notches for what is acceptable.

5. The Internet already is being utilized as the initial step in launching a new mission. The old model called for sending a mission-developer pastor to a geographically defined place to plant a new mission. That model was replaced in the 1980s by a new system that identified a precisely defined constituency to be reached. The next step called for bringing together the members of the team who would go out and create the ministries to reach and serve that constituency.

The Internet opened the door to a new model that depends on early self-identification of the constituency to be served. That "virtual" new mission of a couple hundred adults comes together and quickly acquires a powerful voice in selecting the members of that ministry team.

The initial point in that process has shifted from "Where?" to "Who?" to "Self-identification."

6. When horses were used by the clergy for transportation, a pastor could network only with geographically nearby ministers. The automobile enlarged that circle, and ministerial networks usually were built around denominational identity. The Internet has opened the door to the creation of new ministerial networks based on a huge variety of points of commonality. While engaged in sermon preparation, today's pastor can benefit from the comments of ministers participating in an international "chat room" who are studying the same text in preparation for next Sunday's sermon.

A dramatic example of how the Internet can be used to overcome distance is in the education of children. The dropout rate among the high school age children of migrant farm workers was close to 50 percent in the late 1990s. One reason why was because they and their parents left Texas before the end of the school year and felt it was useless to enroll in a public school in the North for a week or two.

In 1999 the United States Department of Education funded a program that enabled fifty of these teenagers to continue their education during the summer via distance learning. Each one of the fifty was given a laptop computer and trained to use it before moving to Montana, Illinois, or New York for the summer. The program had two goals. One was to enable these youth to graduate from high school on schedule. The other was to help them become proficient in the use of a computer. The parents and students signed a commitment covenant that this would be a top priority every day during the summer. One result was that the graduation rate climbed from 50 percent to nearly 90 percent. Equally important, these teenagers mastered a new skill that will open more doors to their future.

7. Once upon a time candidates for the ministry "went away to seminary." Pastors traveled to a distant place for continuing-education events. The combination of the emergence of scores of self-identified teaching churches plus dis-

tance learning has created a new approach for equipping candidates for ordination and for continuing education experiences for congregational leaders. In the twenty-first century, they will tap into the World Wide Web for information. They will travel to teaching churches for continuing-education experiences.

8. The weekly or monthly parish newsletter formerly was edited, reproduced, and mailed out from the church office. The Internet makes it possible to circulate that parish newsletter (currently in type, but by 2004 in an audio-visual format) over the electronic highway and to invite every viewer to be a contributing editor. As they read it, viewers are invited to add news items and announcements. The member in Arizona receives it as quickly as does the member in Iowa.

9. Tim Berners-Lee, the creator of the World Wide Web, explains that his goal was to create the opportunity for creative people to come together and inspire one another with new ideas.[1] In 1998 the five traditional ways of bringing people together to stimulate creativity were one-to-one, face-to-face conversations, the telephone, group meetings (the most expensive choice), mail, and televised interactive sessions. The Internet adds a sixth, but economic pressures will drop group meetings to a distant sixth and move the Internet to the top of the list.

A growing number of contemporary protest movements consisting largely of adults born after 1970 depend heavily on e-mail and the Internet to build a national constituency. Their fellow protestors born in the 1940s nostalgically recall "the good old days" when organizing a national protest movement required a far greater amount of face-to-face contacts.

E-mail and the Internet can be useful in helping strangers become acquaintances. Face-to-face contacts and shared personal experiences are still required for acquaintanceships to grow into tightly knit friendships.

10. The emergence of scores of parachurch organizations created to resource congregations was one of the most important developments of the last half of the twentieth century. The early decades of the twenty-first century will bring a greater variety of customized resources to congregations via the Internet.

11. The Internet will replace traditional television as the most cost effective way to invite strangers to come to your church.

12. For many pastors the most intimidating consequence of the impact of the Internet will be placing a high value on the personal attractiveness of the minister. To some extent this appears to be a return to the 1950s, when the magnetic personality in the pulpit was the central drawing card in many large congregations.

That concept of the parish ministry as a personality cult began to fade away in the last third of the twentieth century. Congregations began to place a high value on visionary leadership, on a high level of skill in interpersonal relationships, and on a sensitive and relevant response to the needs and concerns younger generations brought to church.

The audio-visual facet of the Internet of 2005 once again will reward the attractive and charming personality.

13. The most obvious consequence will be an increase in the level of competition among the churches for future constituents. This will be especially significant in reaching the generations born after 1990 who were reared on the Internet.

14. A related consequence will be the continued erosion of denominational loyalties.

15. Overlapping these consequences will be a continued increase in the number of very large Protestant congregations that average more than eight hundred in residential attendance. These are the congregations with the resources required to be major players in this new game.

At the other end of the size scale will be a continued

increase in the number of Protestant congregations averaging fewer than fifty at worship. One component of this change will be the numerical decline of congregations that formerly averaged fifty to five hundred at worship and have shrunk into the very small church category. A second will be the attractiveness of those small congregations that combine relationships, intimacy, institutional simplicity, an effective expression of being a loving and caring community, nostalgia, and, "You really are missed if you're not here."

A third factor is that the increased cost of the total compensation for a full-time, seminary-trained, and resident pastor is pricing many of the congregations averaging sixty to 125 at worship out of the ministerial marketplace. A few wealthy denominations can afford to offset this by direct and indirect financial subsidies, but most cannot economically justify that.

A fourth, and what may turn out to be the biggest, factor in this anticipated increase in the number of very small Protestant congregations will be the continued growth in the number of house churches. These tend to consist of middle- and upper-class white suburbanites who have grown weary of the internal strife they have experienced in the traditional institutional expressions of the Christian faith. Seven to twenty of them meet weekly in someone's family room for Bible study, prayer, and worship. Television once allowed them to choose from among six to ten preachers for their worship time. The Internet soon will increase that range of choices to several hundred, including the magnetic personality who was the former pastor for several people in that room.

16. While it is the least significant change on this list, the Internet will complicate efforts to maintain membership lists. The categories of 2010 could include active, inactive, shut-in, resident, non-resident, contributing, friends, constituents, baptized, confirmed, former member, Internet member, Internet constituent, Internet contributing con-

stituent, dual affiliation, and combinations of two or three of the above.

17. Television is credited with increasing the level of discontent among the residents of poor nations. In the 1950s, when these residents compared their lot in life with their kinsfolk and their neighbors, they evaluated themselves as happy. Residents of Germany, Yugoslavia, and Nigeria, despite huge differences in per capita income, were equally happy.

Thirty years later, parallel research studies reported that high-income adults clearly were happier than low-income persons. With but a few exceptions, residents of rich nations were happier than residents of poor nations.[2] The conclusion was that television now enabled the residents of poor nations to compare their standard of living with that of the residents of rich nations. The result is dissatisfaction.

Television in America already is producing similar consequences as parishioners compare their congregation with what they see on television. The Internet will increase that dissatisfaction as congregational leaders contrast the cost and value of resources they receive over the Internet with the cost and quality of resources they receive from traditional suppliers.

"Why can't we do it the way that church does it on the Internet?" will be a question congregational leaders will hear repeatedly in the years ahead.

One response is, "We can't. We do not have the necessary resources." Another response will be a reluctant, "Well, I guess if we're going to survive, we'll have to be more creative and more innovative and offer people more choices."

Television turned out to be a powerful force for change in the poor countries of the world. The World Wide Web will turn out to be a powerful force for change in all institutions in every country.

18. The most delicate and challenging consequence of the

growth of the World Wide Web can possibly be summarized in one word. That word is anonymity.

Unlike the telephone, both radio and television share an advantage that is greatly prized by many people. This is the anonymity of the recipient of the message. That enables a person to experience the worship service via television without risking the potential nuisance of being pressured to "come back next week" or to receive an unwelcome telephone call or knock on the door.

The Internet has come along and virtually wiped out the limitations of geographical distance. The Internet makes it easy to buy a book without going to a bookstore or to purchase common stocks without going to a broker or to reserve an airline ticket without going to a travel agent's office. The Internet makes it easy for a man, without being seen by anyone, to watch a woman take off her clothes. The Internet makes it possible for a person to enroll in a class without ever having face-to-face contact with either the instructor or other students. "Surfing the net" has become an attractive way for millions of people to kill two or three hours every day without risking any investment of their identity.

One big difference between radio and television is in the words hear and experience. Radio enables one to hear what is happening in a place far, far away. Television, like motion pictures, enables one to experience it.

One limitation of radio and television is that both represent one-way communication. A second limitation is that both encourage a passive role for the recipient of the message. A third is that both encourage individual, rather than group, involvement among the recipients of the message.

A serious limitation of television is that the reliance on the visual images tends to oversimplify the contents of the message. Radio is a better channel for communicating complex messages. Radio also has the advantage that, at least until recently, the imagination of a human being could create better visual images than could be transmitted by television.

The Internet has come along and it offers to replace the one-way communication of radio and television with an interactive, but distant and even anonymous, role for the individual.

What will be the result? Will worshiping communities attract people by their unique capability to combine meaningful relationships with other people with experiential worship, challenging learning opportunities built around face-to-face interaction, and distinctive experiences that cannot be duplicated in cyberspace?

Or is our culture training today's eight-year-olds to place a high value on anonymity, impersonal and distant relationships, privacy, and customized schedules?

What are today's eight-year-olds being taught as the criteria to use in choosing a church home? In 1910 eight-year-olds were taught that geographical proximity, kinship ties, and denominational affiliation were important criteria in choosing a church. The eight-year-olds of 1970 were taught that none of those are really important. What will the Internet of 2010 teach the church shoppers of 2030 are the important criteria in choosing an opportunity for the corporate worship of God?

19. What records are kept in the church office? A common requirement of the early years of the twentieth century was a big thick book. In it were recorded the dates and names for all baptisms, new members received, weddings, funerals, and the arrival and departure of ministers.

File folders often included a year-by-year collection of worship bulletins, parish newsletters, annual budgets and financial reports, minutes of congregational meetings, and similar papers.

In the 1990s that collection often was expanded to include videotapes of a variety of events, ceremonies, anniversaries, and celebrations.

Today the church office may be the repository for check-lists filled out by individual members describing what they want to happen at their death and memorial service; a computer disk filled with the names, birth dates, and addresses of each member; a computerized data base of the non-resident constituents; videotapes of aged members who want to offer one last word to the folks who gather at their memorial service; that congregation's license for projecting copyrighted material on a screen; plus an array of electronic equipment for access to the information highway.

20. Finally, as the presidential campaigns and legal battles of November and December 2000 illustrated so clearly, the Internet already has demonstrated that it is an effective and low-cost channel for raising money. For those congregations, parachurch organizations, resource centers, and regional judicatories that bring both an inclination and the necessary skills to this opportunity, the Internet could become the largest single source of money year after year. Obviously the greatest success will come from appeals for designated contributions to attractive causes.

While not offered as an exhaustive list, these examples suggest that the impact of the Internet in the twenty-first century will be at least as great as the impact of the widespread ownership of privately owned motor vehicles and the easy access to television were in the twentieth century.

CHAPTER FIFTEEN

FROM THE WEDDING BUSINESS TO A MARRIAGE MINISTRY?

"You're asking why we are members here?" replied a woman in her late thirties. "That's an easy question. We were married here. My folks decided to move to this town right after I finished my junior year in high school, and they chose this church. I was a regular attendee for only two years before I left to go to the university. After graduation, I got a job in the state capital. That's when I met the man who became my husband. At the time neither one of us had an active church relationship, but I wanted to be married in church. It also pleased my parents that I chose to be married here. Shortly after we were married, my husband was offered a post-graduate fellowship in Michigan. So we moved there, and I found a job with the county. I quit working a few weeks before our first baby was born. The years rolled by, and we had two more children. After twelve years in Michigan, my husband got a promotion, which meant moving back here. By that time my parents had retired and moved to the Sunbelt, so we didn't have any kinship ties here. After we were settled, we started looking for a church home, and, since we had been married here, this one was at the top of our list. The minister who had married us had moved on, but we were favorably impressed with the current pastor and didn't look any further. All three of our kids were excited to discover this was the church in which their parents had been married. All five of us were surprised and delighted to discover our wedding picture on one wall of the fellowship hall. There must be two hundred 8" x 10" color photographs on that wall. That custom was started by the minister who married us. There is no fee for use of the building. The only charge is honoraria for the staff, including the organist, pastor, and custodian, plus that 8" x 10" color picture of the wedding couple. When I saw those pictures on the wall, I felt like I was coming home. More than a dozen of my friends are in pictures on that wall. What was important to my husband, who didn't know any of those people, and to our children was that our picture was on that wall. When you see your own picture on the wall, it makes you feel like you belong there."

The current pastor explained, "Our critics complain that we're nothing more than a wedding chapel. This church has a center aisle, an excellent pipe organ, plenty of parking, and a very large fellowship hall, which is next to the sanctuary and is a wonderful place for receptions. The wedding pictures on that long wall are a great conversation starter for guests. We have lots of women who came for the wedding of a friend and decided this is where they want to be married.

"Most churches in this community require that either the bride or the groom come from a member family or that the couple be regular worshipers for at least a few months or that they complete a premarital counseling program," continued this pastor.

"We don't have any of those requirements. We do require a two-hour planning session with our wedding counselor on what is acceptable here in terms of cameras and other details, but that's it. I meet with the couple for a half hour at the end of that two-hour session and, of course, I usually officiate at the ceremony. But we do have an open door for guest ministers to do that."

"Most of today's pastors are not as open as you appear to be on this issue," I observed.

"That's true," came the quick reply, "and as I told you earlier, we are widely criticized as being too open. Several churches here in town charge anywhere between $500 and $1,200 for use of the building if neither bride nor groom comes from that congregation. Others limit weddings to member families. I try to explain that we believe in relational evangelism. One time to approach the unchurched is when they are on a self-identified religious pilgrimage. Another is at a change in their life cycle, such as a death, a birth, a wedding, or a divorce or when the children are ready for Sunday school. Our open-door policy on weddings is one component of our larger strategy of relational evangelism. Every year we have two or three couples who have just moved here, and they pick us for their new church home because they had been married here earlier. We also welcome a few new members every year who continue to live here after marriage, and our open-door policy on marriage was the beginning of the relationship that motivated them to worship with us after they returned from the honeymoon."

A few months later, a pastor in another city explained, "We used to be in the wedding business here. In the typical year I officiated at two to three dozen weddings, in about half of which neither the bride nor the groom had had any previous relationship with this congregation. We required three two-hour premarital counseling sessions with each couple. That added up to about two hundred hours every year. When you add in the time for the wedding, the picture taking, and the reception, I realized I was spending the equivalent of five or six weeks every year on weddings. That's a lot of time!"

"How have you changed?" I inquired.

"This is my nineteenth year here, and I have tried to keep up with what happened to all the people I married," reflected this pastor. "I found that about one-third of those earlier marriages had ended in divorce within a dozen years after the wedding. That is consistent with national statistics for church weddings. I also read that premarital counseling is far less influential than I had been taught in seminary. So three years ago we decided to abandon the wedding business and replace it with a marriage ministry."

"What does that mean?" I interrupted.

"About three-and-a-half years ago we welcomed a new associate minister who had been married a month earlier. That August our new associate began to offer a Sunday morning class. It runs from eleven o'clock to about one-thirty and includes a light lunch. That allows the members of the class to attend the nine-thirty worship service. The class is designed for newlyweds and for engaged couples planning to be married within the next several months. The theme is how to build a happy and enduring marriage. Once or twice a month an outside expert is brought in to cover a specific topic, and the next two or three weeks are reflection and discussion time for what has been presented. Everyone is asked to make a nine-month commitment to that class from mid-August to late May, but we do allow newcomers to join the class through October."

"What have you learned?" I asked.

"We've learned four lessons," explained the pastor. "First, that 150-minute time including eating together as well as sharing intimate concerns creates a closely knit group. Several times a year most or all of the members spend Saturday at the wedding of a couple in the class. Those shared experiences reinforce the cohesion of the group.

"Second, to our surprise, none of the classes have disbanded in May. The vast majority want to continue as an adult class in the Sunday school. That first class insisted that they be able to keep their same room, and that caused some problems; but we worked it out. We now have three new and closely knit adult classes in our Sunday school that we never planned on. In addition, our new class for engaged couples and recent newlyweds begins this next August. That explains why we built a $400,000 addition two years ago. When it works, creativity costs money!

"Third, we discovered that it is extremely difficult for a new couple, unless both are exceptionally gregarious and persistent, to join one of these classes in the second or third year of its existence. That year of intense, intimate, and shared experiences becomes a high and exclusionary wall. It is impossible, of course, for an individual to come in alone and be fully accepted. Two or three have tried, but the rejection caused them to go elsewhere.

"Fourth, and most important, we're now making the next transition. We abandoned the wedding business we were in for nearly sixteen years and replaced it with a marriage ministry. Eight months ago we launched the next phase, which is a ministry with couples with a new baby. We schedule this for Tuesday evenings with mothers and their babies and Thursday evenings with fathers and the babies."

"Why don't you make it a family evening for the couple and that new baby?" I wondered aloud.

"Simple," explained the pastor. "Our Tuesday and Thursday evening ministries include many couples who have been married for several years. While they do have a new baby as the point of commonality, more than half have an older child in the family. Sometimes this is a child from a former marriage. Our schedule enables one parent to be home with the older child. Second, we plan to continue it for couples when baby number two or number three arrives. Third, and most important, we wanted to start new groups that would be completely open to newcomers. Most of the couples in this Tuesday/Thursday evening ministry never were in any of the classes for newlyweds. These are overlapping ministries in terms of the constituency, but they are separate and focus on two different stages of the life cycle.

"We have not completely abandoned the wedding business. I still officiate at several weddings every year, but most of our weddings now come out of that class for engaged couples and newlyweds, and, of course, my associate officiates at nearly all those. We now have a solid marriage ministry, and we're well into developing what I expect will become a larger ministry with families with very young children. In a couple of years we will need to transform our present ministry with elementary-school aged children into a package of ministries with families with that age cohort."

"Why wait?" I challenged.

"Staffing," was the immediate response. "A few years ago we added our first full-time associate minister. A year ago we added a one-third-time grandmother who is a superb musician to staff our ministries with families with very young children. That is organized around the power of motion and music-based learning.[1] Two years ago we had to add a one-story addition with four classrooms and one large multipurpose room, plus restrooms and two offices. We're still paying for that. That means it will be two to three years before we can staff an expansion of our ministries with families that include elementary aged children. An attractive and exciting marriage ministry has lots of long-term consequences."

A Bit of Speculation

At this writing it appears that one of the most significant and potentially divisive societal changes in the early years of the twenty-first century will focus on the relationships of two adults who choose to live together.

Back in the 1950s most of those arrangements fell into one of the following six categories.[2]

1. Husband/wife couples who were married in a religious ceremony licensed by the state.

2. Husband/wife couples who were married in a civil ceremony licensed by the state.

3. A man and a woman who were living together in what was identified as a "common law marriage."

4. An unmarried man living with an unmarried woman (but this included only seven out of every one thousand couples living together).

5. Homosexual couples living as one family unit.

6. Three or more adults living in a polygamous relationship.

The last three arrangements included a relatively small number of adults.

In 2015 that list of alternative relationships probably will have grown to at least seventeen, plus polygamy.

1. Husband/wife couples married in a religious ceremony that requires participation in a premarital counseling or learning experience.

2. Ditto, but without the premarital counseling requirement.

3. Ditto number 1, but the religious ritual will not include the vow of "until death do us part."

4. Ditto number 2, but omission of the above vow.

5. Homosexual couples in a holy union that is not licensed by the state but is celebrated in a house of worship with a clergyperson officiating.

6. Ditto above, but celebrated in a private setting, not in a house of worship.

7. Ditto number 5, but a relationship licensed by the state and celebrated in a house of worship.

8. Ditto above, but not in a house of worship.

9. Husband/wife who were married in a civil ceremony without required premarital counseling.

10. Husband/wife couples married in a civil ceremony following premarital counseling for which the state provided a financial incentive or a financial subsidy. (By early 2001 a dozen states were offering these financial subsidies.)

11. Homosexual couples united in a state-licensed civil ceremony that provides the legal benefits of marriage.

12. Heterosexual couples united in a state-licensed civil ceremony that provides the legal benefits of marriage, but also includes a low-cost and simple dissolution provision if (a) the couple does not have dependent children and (b) both parties willingly sign a termination agreement that is included in the original contract.

13. Unmarried heterosexual couples who are living together without children and who have chosen not to have either a civil or a religious marriage ceremony. Between 1960 and 2000 the number of couples in this category increased sevenfold.

14. Unmarried homosexual couples who are living together but have chosen not to have either a civil or a religious ceremony.

15. Ditto 13, but with dependent children.

16. Ditto 13, 14, and 15, but, thanks to a flexible employer and changes in state and federal legislation, able to enjoy all the legal benefits, but none of the liabilities, of being married.

17. When applying for a civil license to marry, couples will be given a choice between (a) a low-commitment option that includes a relatively simple provision for dissolution of the compact and (b) a high-commitment version that requires premarital counseling and marriage education plus a far more difficult process for termination of the marriage.

This is far from a complete list of alternative arrangements and completely ignores the arrangements that may be chosen by divorced or widowed adults or retirees or high school and college students. It also ignores the growing number of prenuptial agreements on the future disposition of assets and liabilities. This list also does not include alternatives that may emerge over the judicial interpretation of the "Full faith and credit" clause in Section 1 of Article IV of the United States Constitution, which requires each state to honor the public acts and records of all other states.

Five Trends

The point of this list of seventeen arrangements is to illustrate five trends.

First, many states are encouraging marriage education in hopes of reducing the divorce rate. During the 1990s welfare reform was chosen by many elected public officials as a politically attractive way to create a better world for children. The first years of the twenty-first century will be marked by a parallel effort in what is called marriage education. Since children are the primary victims of divorce, one way to make it a better world for children is to increase the proportion of marriages that are happy and enduring experiences for all involved.

The big unknown is whether the churches will be leaders or laggards in this effort.

Second, religious institutions and the clergy usually are invited, but not required, to be active participants in these state-initiated efforts.

Third, and most important, the traditional American view of marriage as a religious ceremony including a lifelong commitment by a man and a woman to each other no longer is the universally accepted norm.

One possibility is that the term "marriage" will be reserved for religious rituals, while "wedding" and/or "union" will be the term used to describe civil and other nonreligious relationships.

Fourth, the number of heterosexual couples seeking the

163

legal benefits of marriage, but without the requirement of a religious ceremony, already greatly exceeds the number of homosexual couples seeking a civil union. (In 1999 France created an "easy in, easy out" legal partnership for childless adults who seek the civil and legal benefits of being married but do not want to be burdened with all the baggage of marriage. For many heterosexual couples, that has turned out to be an interim stage between "living together" and marriage.)

Fifth, in all probability, changes in state laws that expand the range of legal arrangements for adults who choose to live together will come first in the Northeast followed by the West, the Midwest, and the South.

This will lead to divisive battles in those religious bodies that choose to have one set of rules that control all the clergy and all the congregations within that body. The big battles will be between those who demand nationwide uniformity and those who advocate a federalist approach that allows each regional judicatory to develop a set of policies and practices that are in harmony with the laws of the states included in that regional judicatory.

Those religious traditions that place a high level of trust in congregational leaders to design their own policies and practices will find it easy to adjust to this rapidly expanding list of alternatives available to adults who choose to live together.

On the other hand, for those denominations that place a high value on the need to regulate the policies and practices of both congregations and the clergy, this expanding list of alternatives, with its sharp regional differences in what are legally acceptable practices, will provide grist for the agendas at their national conventions. One item on that agenda will be to decide on how high the bar should be for a couple wanting to be united in a religious ceremony by a clergyperson within the building housing a congregation affiliated with that religious tradition. Another item on that agenda will be to decide what is acceptable language. Which of these terms will be acceptable? Wedding? Marriage? Sacrament? Partnership? Holy union? Pact? Prenuptial agreement? Man and wife? Spouse? Lovers? Covenant? Contract? Civil union?

Every few years it will be necessary to amend or revise the regulatory policies adopted at previous sessions. These new agendas will make it easier to explain to the constituency why these are important meetings.

The Road to a Blended Society?

Finally, it appears that the recent emphasis on multiculturalism in high schools, colleges, and universities; in residential living; in employment practices; in recreation and sports; in television programming; and in congregational life are combining to create more intercultural marriages. In 1980, 3 percent of all married couples of all ages were in ethnically or racially mixed marriages. By 1998, that proportion had grown to 5 percent and probably will approach 15 percent by 2020.

In 1998 one-fifth of all Asian-ancestry wives in the United States were married to non-Asian men. Two-thirds of all married Latinos in America in 1998 who had completed at least one year of college were married to a non-Latino. One out of eight of all American-born married blacks in 1998 with at least one year of college were married to a non-black spouse.

Multicultural enrollment in institutions of higher education and in the workplace may be the two most productive means of creating a blended multicultural society. The fears of the racial segregationists of the 1950s are becoming the reality of the twenty-first century!

CHAPTER SIXTEEN

HOW DO YOU CLASSIFY CHURCHES?

When I was a Methodist pastor in Wisconsin back in the 1950s, some of us divided Christian congregations into two categories—them and us. "Them" referred to the two dominant religious traditions, Catholic and Lutheran, which accounted for approximately four out of five churchgoers on the typical Sunday. To identify ouselves, we coined the seven syllable term "Non-LutheranProtestant."

Concurrently Will Herberg published his popular book, *Protestant-Catholic-Jew.*[1] Herberg contended that until recently Americans had identified themselves by their national ancestry. After World War II, however, younger generations began to identify themselves by their religious affiliation.

In retrospect, however, it now is clear that the number-one line of demarcation among American Christian churches in the 1950s was skin color. That was the highest wall separating both congregations and denominations. While it is not as high as it was in the 1950s, skin color continues today to be the least flexible variable in classifying churches.

The past half century has brought a rapidly growing variety of systems that are used to classify churches. The guiding assumption is that when human beings are confronted with a huge number of objects or people or institutions, dividing that large group into smaller units makes it easier to comprehend reality. We all rely on classification systems. We classify people by age, marital status, education, race, ethnicity, income, social status, citizenship, language, and other variables. We also classify dogs, retail stores, dwellings, candidates for the presidency, restaurants, physicians, automobiles, major league sports teams, food, hospitals, motion pictures, birds, and books.

A Denominational Perspective

The majority of Christian congregations in the United States carry a denominational affiliation. Frequently that denominational culture influences the priorities, policies, and practices of those congregations. Therefore, it may be useful to begin by introducing one system that can be used to classify denominations.

I. The Western European Reformation Coalition

This category includes the six denominations (Evangelical Lutheran Church in America, the Episcopal Church, the United Church of Christ, the Presbyterian Church [U.S.A.], the Reformed Church in America, The Moravian Church) that have been coming closer together in recent years.

This group also includes a long list of other denominations that carry a western European heritage, including various Mennonite bodies, the Christian Reformed Church, several Lutheran denominations, the Orthodox traditions, and others.

II. American-born Black Churches

This group of churches includes the African Methodist Episcopal Church, the African Methodist Zion Church, the Christian Methodist Episcopal Church, the Church of God in Christ, the National Baptist Convention of America, Inc., the National Baptist Convention, U.S.A., Inc., the

Progressive National Baptist Convention, Inc., plus scores of pentecostal, charismatic, independent, Church of God, and other predominantly black denominations.

III. Made-in-America Religious Traditions

This huge and growing category includes hundreds of religious traditions and movements that originated within what is now the United States of America. Among the largest of these are the Assemblies of God, the Church of Jesus Christ of the Latter-day Saints, the Reorganized Church of Jesus Christ of Latter-day Saints, the Seventh-day Adventist Church, the Church of God of Anderson, the Southern Baptist Convention, the Universal Fellowship of Metropolitan Community Churches, the Presbyterian Church of America, the Evangelical Presbyterian Church, the Congregational Christian component of the United Church of Christ, the Church of the Nazarene, the Conservative Baptist Association, the Christian Church (Disciples of Christ), the Churches of Christ, Conservative Judaism, and Reconstructionist Judaism.

IV. The Immigrant Tradition

Many of the Christian bodies in this category are well along in the process of being Americanized, but still retain a substantial western European heritage. Examples of this type include the Evangelical Covenant Church, the Evangelical Free Church in America, a couple of the Mennonite traditions, the Wisconsin Evangelical Lutheran Synod, Reformed Judaism, and a few Orthodox Jewish congregations.

Thousands of other congregations, however, are clearly immigrant churches and include the Hutterites, the Amish, plus Asian, African, Mexican, Latino, Caribbean, Portuguese, Islam, Buddhist, and other traditions.

V. Institutionally Conservative

This category includes those religious traditions that are institutionally organized around a strong distrust of local leadership, a powerful resistance to change, and a highly centralized command and control system of governance. The two largest examples in this category are the Roman Catholic Church and The United Methodist Church.

Among other uses, this fivefold system of categories helps to explain some of the more recent cooperative ventures in ministry across traditional boundaries. This system also helps to explain why other proposals for interchurch cooperation have moved so slowly.

Most important, however, this system can be helpful in understanding why some religious traditions are open to certain changes while others resist similar proposals for change. For example, most of the made-in-America religious traditions are exceptionally open to complete local control of the decision-making process. By contrast, the institutionally conservative religious traditions and, to a lesser extent, those in the coalition of western European Reformation religious bodies tend to be more resistant to local control. Likewise, the first-generation immigrant congregations tend to resist the Americanization of their American-born children, while that usually is a minor issue in the third-generation immigrant churches.

44 Systems

It is relatively easy to identify a respectable number of systems used to classify religious congregations. Several are old, a few are new, and some are far more useful than others. That respectable number, of course, is forty-four.[2] What are they? Which do you believe are the most useful? This observer's choices for the sixteen most useful are marked with a •.

169

•1. *Skin Color?* In the United States this continues to be the most widely followed system. At least a few readers would prefer to use the word "race," but in American history that has been an ambiguous term with changing definitions.

•2. *Protestant, Catholic, or Jewish?* This continues to be widely used, but should be expanded to include Islam and other religions.

•3. *Language?* This was a widely used line of demarcation in the 1870–1940 era. In recent years, language once again has become a highly relevant system.

4. *First Day or Seventh Day?* One of the basic dividing lines in American Christianity for several decades separated those Christian congregations that regularly gathered for the corporate worship of God on the seventh day of the week from those that gathered on the first day. One of the most radical, but least controversial, changes in American Protestantism came as a growing number of first-day churches added a Saturday evening or Thursday evening or Monday night worship service to the weekly schedule. In at least a couple of dozen first-day congregations, the most highly attended service is on Saturday evening.

•5. *Western European or Made in America?* One of the most significant changes in American Christianity during the second half of the twentieth century was the gradual decline in the proportion of churchgoers who chose a congregation affiliated with a religious tradition that represented a western European religious heritage (Roman Catholic, Presbyterian, Episcopal, Lutheran, Reformed, Methodist, etc.). This was more than offset by the increase in the proportion choosing a made-in-America religious tradition (Independent, Assemblies of God, Four Square Gospel, Bible Church, Latter-Day Saints, etc.).

6. *Liberal or Conservative?* This line between the theologically liberal and theologically conservative congregations was widely applied to various denominational systems in the 1900–1970 era. In recent years it has turned out to be more use-

ful in identifying differences within a particular denominational tradition. The intradenominational differences between liberal and conservative have become more significant than the interdenominational differences on this scale. By 1990, however, both words were becoming increasingly confusing because of the absence of widely accepted definitions.

7. *Rural or Urban?* This became a widely used system in the 1950s with the migration of rural residents to urban America. By 1960, however, it began to be replaced by metropolitan or non-metropolitan. Today so many urbanites have moved to rural America and so many center-city residents were born into a rural environment that the system is nearly obsolete.

8. *Cooperative or Non-Cooperative?* This was a popular system during the rise of ecumenism in the 1950s and 1960s. This line separated those churches that were interested in cooperating with one another from those that preferred a unilateral approach. The recent shift from denominations to congregations as the basic building blocks for interchurch cooperation has reduced the value of this system as a predictor.

• 9. *How Big?* From this observer's perspective one of the half-dozen most useful systems is to classify congregations by size using average worship attendance as the yardstick to measure size.[3]

Size can be a highly useful reference point in making decisions on staffing, specialized outreach ministries, real estate, finances, schedules, governance, interchurch cooperation, and music.

• 10. *Which Person of the Holy Trinity?* If one examines the hymns, the wording of the prayers, and the content of the sermon, most congregations fall into one of three categories. The smallest group places a great emphasis on God the Creator. The largest focus more heavily on Jesus the Savior. A third group exalts the Holy Spirit. For many of today's church shoppers, this is one of the most influential classification systems.

171

11. *Memorial or Real Presence?* In one group of churches, the real presence of Christ in the elements of Holy Communion is a central doctrine. In others, that is a decision left to each worshiper. In many, the Lord's Supper is described as a memorial. Once upon a time that was a very high wall separating one Protestant tradition from another.

12. *Who Is the Enemy?* For many American Protestant religious bodies, a powerful central organizing principle was to identify a common external enemy and organize against that enemy. Among the common external enemies were Roman Catholicism, heresy, alcoholic beverages, the devil, ignorance, slavery, the pope, divorce, white racism, immigrants, the Trilateral Commission, drugs, desegregation, and homosexuality.

In recent years it has become more difficult to achieve widespread agreement on the identification of a common external enemy. In several denominations this vacuum has been filled by a search for a common internal enemy. One difference is that identifying a common external enemy can be a powerful unifying tactic. The search for a common internal enemy, however, usually is a highly divisive tactic.

13. *Infant or Believer's Baptism?* What is the doctrine of baptism in that congregation? Do they baptize infants? Or do they insist that a person be old enough to make an informed decision? Or is that an option left to the parents?

14. *Instrumental Music?* This wall has almost disappeared, but thousands of congregations still prohibit instrumental music in worship. Many others limit it to the piano or organ. A rapidly growing number are completely open on this issue.

15. *Psalter or Hymnal or Neither?* For many decades a clear line of demarcation was between those congregations that sang out of the psalter and those that used a hymnal. As that wall has crumbled, the new dividing line is between those congregations that operate on the assumption that worshipers sing better with their chins down and using

hymnals versus those that believe singing with the chin up is a more comfortable posture and that project the words on a screen.

16. *Volunteer or Paid Pastor?* For economic as well as theological reasons, tens of thousands of American Protestant congregations, especially immigrant and black churches, have relied on a pastor who is financially self-supporting.

The tripling in the size of the average Protestant congregation during the twentieth century plus affluence encouraged many of these to switch to a part-time or full-time paid pastor.

In recent years, however, that pendulum has swung back. Today the number of small mainline Protestant congregations and independent house churches with either one volunteer or a team of volunteers filling the role of pastor is increasing. Many of these volunteers possess two or three or four or five earned academic degrees. Distance learning will increase this inventory of volunteers sharply during the next few decades.

• 17. *Clergy or Lay Led?* For most of the first three hundred years of American Protestantism, the clergy were dominant. They determined policies and set the standards. The twentieth century brought an expansion of the role of the laity.

Today it is easy to find very large and rapidly growing congregations in which a small number of lay elders, often with one pastor as a member of that team, make all the important decisions. It is easier, however, to find a far, far larger number of smaller congregations in which the clergy, both at the congregational and the denominational levels, are far, far more powerful than the laity in policy making. Some of the laity describe it as the difference between internal local and lay control and external, clergy-dominated control.

This has become an important line of demarcation for younger generations as they search for a new church home.

•18. *Immigrant or American-Born?* This was an extremely important line of demarcation in American Christianity in the 1870–1930 era. The radical cutback in immigration made it an increasingly obsolete system by 1960. Today it is one of the half dozen most useful categories.

The next stage, of course, already has arrived and consists of congregations of the American-born adult children of immigrant parents. One simple consequence is that we now see Korean congregations, Korean American congregations, and American congregations that are composed largely of worshipers of Korean ancestry.

19. *Sunday School or Not?* For nearly two centuries Sunday school was an essential component of the Sunday morning schedule for almost all Baptist, Methodist, Christian, and Presbyterian congregations as well as for many others. The shift in recent years from an emphasis on teaching to a focus on learning has resulted in many congregations eliminating Sunday school completely and scheduling learning experiences at other times during the week.

•20. *Christian School or Public School?* For more than a century Roman Catholic, Lutheran, Seventh-day Adventist, Christian Reformed, and a few other traditions placed a high value on providing weekday Christian school for children in that parish. Most of the Baptists, Presbyterians, Methodists, and others were increasingly militant advocates of the public schools.

The emergence of segregationist academies in the South in the 1950s and 1960s began to change that pattern. The decision by many elected public officials to enroll their children in private schools began to legitimate that choice for liberals who had been defenders of the public schools. The rise of home schooling and the deterioration of many public school systems has encouraged younger parents to take a second look at this issue. The recent rapid increase in the number of black children enrolled in Christian schools, both Roman Catholic and Protestant, has transformed the political climate. The emergence of tax-funded charter schools has created another option.

By 2001 it was increasingly easy to find independent and mainline Protestant congregations, both black and white, operating a Christian school as one component of a much larger ministry with families with young children.

•*21. Projected Visual Imagery?* Among parish pastors Robert Schuller stands out as the pioneer innovator in the use of television. Schuller has demonstrated that television can be the most effective tool to transform what otherwise would have been a regional congregation into a national church and eventually into a global presence.

Where it was economically feasible, television also turned out to be the most effective channel for inviting strangers to come to your church.

By 1996, the use of videotapes and film clips was beginning to replace oral illustrations in sermons as well as a powerful component of the learning process.

By 2001, the use of visual images in communication had become one of the half dozen most meaningful systems in classifying churches.

22. *Denominational or Independent or Dual Affiliation?* The old question was, "Which denomination are you affiliated with?" By 1970 the question was, "Is this a denominationally affiliated congregation or an independent church?" By 1990 the question included, ". . . or do you have a dual affiliation?"

One alternative before several Protestant denominations in the twenty-first century is, "Do we divide or do we try to stay together?" Another alternative could be to permit congregations to have full affiliation with the denomination they have been a member of for decades and also enjoy full affiliation with a denomination with which that congregation finds a greater degree of compatibility. This could be the win-win response to the threat of schism.

On another front, this already is the choice of several historically white denominations as part of a larger strategy to become a multicultural body. One common example is the black congregation that is a member of one of the black Baptist denominations and is dually affiliated with the Southern Baptist Convention or the American Baptist churches.

The lesson is that the old either/or option is being replaced by the both/and choice.

While less widely discussed, several million Protestant churchgoers claim membership in two different congregations. The Internet will stimulate an increase in the number of two-church members!

23. *When Do the Visitors First Appear?* When do the majority of first-time visitors come to your meeting place? For the overwhelming majority of Christian congregations in the United States, the answer is weekend worship.

For many of the larger congregations with a relatively young constituency, the answer is more likely to be, "Sometime between Monday morning and Saturday noon." They first appear at the Christian day school or at a Monday evening intensive 150-minute adult Bible study group or to help pioneer a new Tuesday evening mutual support group or in an afterschool program or at one of a score or more weekday and weeknight ministries events or summer programs.

•24. *Growing or Shrinking?* The emergence of the church growth movement in the 1960s added a useful system for classifying congregations. Is your congregation growing in size or shrinking in numbers? How do you measure that? By membership figures? Baptisms? Worship attendance? Professions of faith? What has been the trend over the past five years? Since the arrival of the present pastor?

•25. *Take Care of Our Own or Evangelize?* The church growth movement also has encouraged a second classification system. One group of congregations makes decisions on schedules, the allocation of staff time and energy, the use of building space, the priorities on the time of volunteers, and proposals for change on the basis of taking better care of current members. A smaller group of congregations makes those decisions on the basis of what will strengthen the evangelistic outreach.

•26. *Parking: Surplus or Deficit?* For at least three-quarters of all Protestant congregations averaging more than 125 at worship, a crucial line of demarcation separates those congregations that own a surplus of off-street parking from those that own little or no off-street parking.

This may cease to be a significant variable if and when the price of gasoline goes above $7 per gallon.

27. *Neighborhood or Regional?* The neighborhood elementary school, the neighborhood grocery, the neighborhood motion picture theater, the neighborhood insurance agent, the neighborhood church, and the neighborhood drugstore were valuable assets in urban America as recently as the 1950s.

Most were replaced by the end of the twentieth century.

This has created four categories of congregations in this classification system: (a) the ex-neighborhood church with a commuting constituency, (b) the ex-neighborhood church that has been transformed into a regional congregation, (c) the numerically shrinking neighborhood church, and (d) the thriving neighborhood church with a precisely and narrowly defined niche.

28. *What Is the Self-image?* Instead of building a self-image around a neighborhood constituency and/or a denominational affiliation, many congregations have chosen a self-image as (a) an extended and caring family fellowship or (b) a program church or (c) a church with a narrowly and precisely stated belief system or (d) one built around the personality of the long-tenured pastor or (e) a seven-day-a-week ministry or (f) a mission-driven congregation or (g) a group based on characteristics (race, language, nationality,

177

age, marital status, sexual orientation, etc.) of the primary constituency or (h) the advocate for justice for the poor, the oppressed, the helpless, the needy, and the recent immigrant.

The basic generalization is that the higher the density of the population and/or the greater the number of churches per square mile, the more important it is for each congregation to project an intentional and precisely defined self-image.

29. *How Old?* If a congregation has been worshiping God in the same room for more than forty years, it probably either (a) is experiencing numerical decline or (b) has reinvented itself and in that process designed a new ministry plan to reach a new constituency.

Never before in American church history have there been so many congregations that are vulnerable to this "forty-year syndrome."

30. *Have You Paid?* In The United Methodist Church, and to a lesser extent in a few other denominations, the most highly visible and regularly used system for classifying congregations is to divide all congregations into two categories. The first consists of those that have paid their denominational dues in full and/or on schedule. The second includes those that are delinquent in their payments to denominational headquarters.

•31. *Memories or Vision?* What drives the decision-making processes? In one group of congregations the answer is largely memories of the past. In a smaller number of churches, the answer is a compelling vision of a new tomorrow.

32. *Own or Rent?* One of the more controversial issues in contemporary American Protestantism has created a new system for classifying congregations. The dominant group places a high value on "owning our own meeting place." A second group is reluctant renters. A third group is comfortable tenants who are convinced, "We must invest those scarce dollars in building the staff to enable us to create a large congregation before we begin to allocate money for

real estate." The smallest group consists of those who are ideologically convinced that renting is the best permanent alternative for the maximum number of dollars to be allocated to ministry and missions.

33. *Low Power Radio?* By 2005 a new system for classifying congregations probably will have emerged. If the Federal Communications Commission prevails over the lobbyists for the large radio chains, one group of congregations will be those that own a licensed low power radio station. The much larger group will be those congregations that have decided that this channel for proclaiming the gospel and witnessing to the Christian faith is not for them.

34. *Experiential or Intellectual?* One of the most interesting systems for classifying churches consists of three groups. One takes an intellectual approach to proclaiming the gospel. That usually includes a presentation-type of worship service. A second places a high priority on an experiential approach. That usually includes participatory worship and a greater reliance on contemporary Christian music.

A small, but growing, third group offers one or more nontraditional experiential worship services plus one or more traditional presentation-type worship services every weekend.

•35. *Send Money or People?* If the goal is the transformation of believers into deeply committed followers of Jesus Christ, this is the most useful system for classifying congregations in this list. (See chapter 10 for an elaboration of this point.)

36. *Law or Grace?* This has replaced the old dichotomy of liberal/conservative as a useful system for classifying congregations, especially if the focus is on generations born after 1960 (see chap. 6).

37. *How Many Choices?* Back in the second quarter of the twentieth century, the societal context was compatible with offering people two choices: take it or leave it. The growing

affluence of the second half of the twentieth century has moved choices from a luxury to an entitlement.

The one big exception are those congregations that are organized around a precisely and narrowly defined belief system and also enjoy a relatively homogeneous constituency. They often thrive by offering two identical worship services on Sunday morning and a relatively limited range of choices in learning experiences, as a volunteer in ministry, and in fellowship opportunities.

The guiding generalization is, The greater the affirmation of demographic diversity and/or theological pluralism, the greater the demand for meaningful choices.

38. *What Is the Role of Women?* For most of American church history, one of the most significant lines of demarcation separating one group of congregations from others has focused on the role of women. In one group of churches the only gender distinctions are on the doors of restrooms. All leadership positions, both lay and ordained, are open to women. At the other extreme are the congregations that severely limit the role of women.

The important lesson on this issue is that the currents of change are all running in the same direction, but at different speeds.

39. *What Is the Congregational/Denominational Relationship?* At one end of this spectrum are the regional judicatories that state clearly that a very high priority is for every congregation to support the denominational goals and budget (see chap. 17).

At the other end of this spectrum are those regional judicatories that are organized to help congregations to define and fulfill their call to ministry.

The currents of change on this issue are running in both directions.

40. *Who Opens the Service?* At one end of this spectrum are the majority of Protestant congregations in which the pastor and/or choir director opens the worship service.

180

At the other end are a small but growing number of congregations in which a worship team of three to fifteen laypersons (most or all of whom are volunteers) opens the service with music, prayer, Scripture, and a high level of congregational participation. The pastor either does not appear or makes only a very brief appearance until after fifteen to twenty-five minutes have passed.

The dominant contemporary trend is to expand the role of the laity in leading worship.

41. *Single-Generational or Multigenerational?* The adult-owned and operated world in the United States of the 1930s and earlier has been eroded gradually by generational separation.

The guiding generalization is that the larger the number of people in that setting, the more likely self-initiated generational separation will occur. This can be seen in church picnics, at motion picture theaters, in restaurants, in large universities, in the recent rapid increase in the number of retirement villages, and in the growing number of Protestant congregations composed largely of a single generation.

The adults in nearly all Protestant churches make it clear that their preference is for a multigenerational constituency. Therefore, that is not the line of demarcation.

In this system of classification, the crucial line of demarcation is **not** between those congregations that are content to be largely single-generation churches and those that want to be multigenerational. The crucial line divides those that are willing to make the changes required to be multigenerational from those that are unwilling. Frequently these changes include the criteria to be used in selecting policymaking and staff members, the design of worship services, priorities in the use of the building, the priority placed on off-street parking, the emphasis placed on evening events, the differences between the high-commitment churches and the low-expectation congregations, and the choice of music.

181

42. *Classical or Contemporary?* One of the easiest classification systems positions those congregations that place a high value on classical Christian music on one side and those that prefer contemporary Christian music on the other side (see chap. 13).

43. *How Do You Invite?* One of the least discussed classification systems divides congregations into four overlapping categories. The least noticed are those congregations that depend largely or entirely on the word-of-mouth messages conveyed by their enthusiastic and deeply committed constituents to invite potential future constituents. A second group places a high value on direct mail, radio, newspaper ads, plastic envelopes hung on doorknobs, telephone calling, and door-to-door visitation. Most of these are primarily invitations to Sunday morning worship. The third group intentionally creates a variety of attractive entry points scattered throughout the week and invites outsiders to come and help pioneer these new ministries. The fourth and largest group consists of those congregations that explain, "We're here. Our doors are open. We welcome anyone and everyone who wants to come and join us in the worship of God."

•44. *Single Site or Multisite?* The most interesting system for classifying congregations also may represent one of the most significant trends of the 1990–2020 era.

Historically in American Christianity, a congregation was identified by (a) its religious tradition; (b) the racial, ancestral, language, social class, educational, or occupational characteristics of the founders; (c) the real estate where that congregation gathered to worship God; and, sometimes, (d) the personality of a long-tenured pastor. The location, size, and cost of the building housing that congregation often ranked near the top of the list of identifying characteristics.

One break with that image came when the congregation had outgrown its meeting place and was faced with the question, "Should we relocate or remain here?" The new answer sometimes was, "Yes." The operational result was to become a two-site congregation with one belief system, one name, one staff, one budget, one governing board, and two locations.

Another break with tradition came when a congregation decided, "Rather than expect people to come here and worship God with us on our turf, we will go to them." This also often turned out to be an effective strategy for transforming what was largely a monocultural congregation into a multicultural parish.

A third break came when larger congregations began to abandon the old model of sponsoring new missions. Instead of identifying money, venturesome members, and perhaps professional staff as the critical "exports" in helping to plant a new mission, a review of past experiences produced a new design. What is the most valuable asset a large church can export to a new mission? A common answer is, How to function effectively as a large congregation!

The best way to provide that asset is not with the discontinuity that usually goes with sending a few score plus families some money. The best way is to become a multisite congregation.[4] With the exception of real estate considerations, this makes it relatively easy to maintain the continuity of the unique culture, the experience, the wisdom, and the insights of that larger church. Instead of sending out one hundred people to launch what will begin as a small church, and thus naturally attract adults who prefer the intimacy and simplicity of a small congregation, the very large congregation averaging 1,200 at three Sunday morning worship services begins with two services at the new site and soon is averaging 900 to 1,500 back at the original site and 700 to 1,000 at the second location. That strategy tends to attract people who seek the quality, the choices, and the teaching of that particular large church, but are reluctant to travel fifteen to thirty miles each way two or three times a week.

While there continues to be powerful ideological support for launching heavily subsidized small missions, economic considerations alone are making the multisite option an increasingly attractive choice.

Why?

At this point the reader may pause and inquire, "Why cut down healthy trees to circulate one more long list?"

This list of forty-four different classification systems is not intended to be exhaustive. It would be easy to expand it to sixty. This list is presented here primarily to introduce five lessons from experience that also answer that "Why?" question.

First, intentionally or unintentionally, every congregational and denominational leader uses some type of system to classify congregations. This list is offered to identify several of the more common as well as some of the more useful.

Second, there is no neutral or value-free system for classifying churches. The higher the level of intentionality in the planning process, the more important it is to select a classification system that is consistent with and supportive of the values and goals of that institution.

A simple way to identify the core values of a congregation is to examine the reporting system. For illustration purposes, I will use an excessively simplistic classification system that includes only five categories. In one group of congregations, the primary central organizing principle is the corporate worship of God. This dominates the planning when the time comes to design a permanent meeting place. Worship is the first priority in the allocation of the pastor's time and energy. In smaller congregations, the only paid program staffer, in addition to the minister, is a part-time choir director. The number-one criterion in selecting a new minister is, "First of all, we want someone who is a good preacher!"

A second category consists of congregations organized around the Sunday school. The Sunday school superintendent is the most influential position for a lay volunteer. If and when the congregation is able to add a second professional to the payroll, that new position probably will be for a director of Christian education.

A third category includes those congregations in which the top priority is taking good care of the members. If and when a second staff position is created, it probably will be for a part-time retired minister who excels in pastoral care. When the current pastor departs, an important factor in choosing a successor will be the plea for a "loving shepherd."

A fourth group of churches consists of those organized around missions. During the past several years a dozen members have responded to the call to become career missionaries. The church organizes and hosts a big missionary conference every year. The first claim on those dollars in the offering plate is for missions.

The fifth category includes those congregations organized around the institutional survival of this congregation meeting in this building on this site. One of the longtime members explains, "We have an obligation to pass this building on to the next generation in better shape than it was when an earlier generation passed it on to us."

What is the highlight or central theme in the annual report of these congregations?

The first group probably will report the average worship attendance for the past year and compare that number with the previous year.

The second group will focus first on Sunday school attendance. The second theme may be to identify and describe the new class(es) organized during the past year.

The annual report of the third group will give prominent space to the name of every member who died during the past year plus a report on the number of births, baptisms, weddings, and funerals. That report also may include the number of hospital and home pastoral calls completed by the minister or the staff.

The fourth group of congregations will devote considerable space to the names and experiences of missionaries related to that church, the number of new missions sponsored, the number of dollars allocated to missions, a tribute to short-term volunteers, and a report on that annual missionary conference.

The fifth group will focus on improvements made to the real estate during the past year, perhaps the names of the volunteers plus words of appreciation for these members, and a report on the dollar cost plus the amount to be raised to pay off the debt.

The moral of this story is that we all tend to count and report on what we believe is truly important.

The regional judicatory that places a high value on theological pluralism may be more comfortable with a system that focuses on the Holy Trinity. This system can be used to identify the congregations affiliated with that denomination that are organized to exalt God the Creator, the number that focus on Jesus the Savior, and those that can be called "Spirit filled." Achieving the goal of theological pluralism within that regional judicatory requires a significant number of congregations in each category.

That same system also can be extremely useful in ministerial placement if the goal is to secure a compatible match between pastor and congregation.

Third, the decision-making process often can be improved if everyone involved begins "on the same page." That cliché includes agreement on the definition of contemporary reality, including the classification systems to describe that particular congregation when compared to other churches.

Fourth, for many congregations the planning process is driven by a new vision of what God is calling that church to be and to do in the years ahead. Agreement on the relevance of two or three systems of classification usually can make it easier to reach agreement on the probable consequences of implementing that vision of a new tomorrow and to communicate that vision to the constituents.

Finally, the choice of a planning model always has a tremendous influence on the data that will be gathered in that process and on the recommendations that emerge from that process. A model built on the scarcity of resources produces a different set of conclusions than the model that assumes an abundance of resources.

Likewise, the choice of a system for classifying congregations usually has a huge impact on the assumptions, data, and goals that are gathered in a denominational planning process.

As congregational leaders define their future roles in a community served by a dozen or more other Christian churches, the system of classification they use will influence the path they believe God is calling their church to follow.

CHAPTER SEVENTEEN

WHO RESOURCES WHOM?

One of the trends in American Christianity during the second half of the twentieth century was a normal, natural, and predictable consequence of the centralization of authority. National denominational agencies began to act on the assumption that they had not only a right but also an obligation to tell the leaders in congregations and regional judicatories what they could and could not do.[1]

This pattern of organizational behavior has been a characteristic of American Catholicism for a long time, and, to a lesser extent, a central component of American Methodism. During the past half century, however, this characteristic of centralized authority began to be expressed more frequently in circles where congregational autonomy had been a historic and accepted concept. That list includes the Lutheran Church-Missouri Synod, the Southern Baptist Convention, and, to a much lesser extent, the United Church of Christ. This permission-withholding expression of authority has long been a part of the polity of several other denominations, including the Presbyterian Church (U.S.A.), the Christian Reformed Church, the Reformed Church in America, and the Evangelical Lutheran Church in America.

A natural consequence of this centralization of authority has been for national agencies to expand their regulatory role, to expect regional and local organizations to resource the national body, and to assume that the regional and local organizations exist to implement the mandates adopted by the national body.

This has been at the heart of the debate over federalism in American civil government during the past half century. Do the states exist to carry out the mandates adopted by Congress? Should the states or the federal government have the primary responsibility for regulating the work of local public school districts? Should the federal income tax system be designed primarily to produce revenue? Or to regulate the behavior of individuals? Or to regulate the policies of corporations? Or to influence the tax policies of states, municipalities, and counties? Or to influence how individuals allocate their discretionary income? Or to encourage or discourage personal savings?

The last quarter of the twentieth century brought an increase in the number of block grants by the federal government as part of a larger trend that recognized and affirmed the differences among states and local communities.

The parallel question in the ecclesiastical arena is, Do congregations exist to resource and help to implement denominational policies and goals? Are denominational agencies called by God to do what congregations cannot or will not or should not do, such as plant new missions or create and fund new institutions like retirement centers? Or to design, staff, and finance specialized ministries? Or to own and operate camps and retreat centers? Or to offer continuing educational experiences for congregational leaders? Or to design, staff, and finance missionary efforts on other continents? Or to produce and distribute printed resources for congregations? Or to examine and ordain candidates for the ministry? Or to create and operate theological schools? Or to preach the gospel via radio, television, and the World Wide Web? Or to collect money from the wealthy and give it to the needy?

One response is that a rapidly growing number of congregations are carrying out most or all of those ministries.

189

Another response is that in today's ecclesiastical world denominational agencies, both national and regional, should exist primarily to provide customized resources for congregations.

During the 1990s the South Carolina Convention of the Southern Baptist Convention and several other regional judicatories adopted what many perceived to be a radical stance. They decided that their guiding principle would be to resource congregations. Instead of measuring "success" by the number of dollars congregations sent to headquarters or the attendance at state convention-sponsored events, they decided that the success of the state convention should be measured by how well each Southern Baptist congregation in South Carolina was doing in defining and fulfilling its mission. The purpose of that state convention was redefined to undergird that new definition of the reason for the existence of the state convention. The organizational structure, the system of governance, the program, the budget, the staffing configuration, and the workload were redefined to be consistent with that reason for existence.

What's the Difference?

An old conceptual framework that was widely used to distinguish one regional judicatory from another was the liberal/conservative line of demarcation. The new line of demarcation reflects purpose and organizational structure. "That regional judicatory is organized on the assumption that it exists to resource congregations and to provide customized help as congregations seek to define their role and to fulfill their mission. This regional judicatory is organized on the assumption that congregations exist to resource and to help implement denominational goals and programs. One consequence is that it can provide some 'one size fits all' help to congregations, but only rarely offer customized services."

190

This new definition of purpose and role also is being adopted by many smaller denominations that include fewer than one thousand congregations. Their size often means that a change of four or five faces in key national staff positions is all that is required to replace the old regulatory role with the new one of resourcing congregations.

In those larger denominations that include more than three thousand congregations,[2] however, the institutional culture, the history, the continued influence of white males who died between 1500 and 2000, the polity, the power of the past, and the bureaucratic structure make it difficult to abandon the comfort that goes with the regulatory role and replace it with the challenge of customized resourcing.

One consequence is that younger generations can be found in disproportionately larger numbers in (a) the independent congregations or (b) congregations affiliated with a religious system designed to resource rather than to regulate.

The Central Issue

From this observer's perspective, the central issue, which also surfaces in other chapters in this book, can be summarized in one word: *Trust*.[3] The regulatory role for denominational agencies is based on the assumption that local leaders, both lay and clergy, cannot be trusted to make wise decisions. Whether they want it or not, people can benefit from the help of the experts. Few will dispute that.

The big dispute is over whether that help should come in the form of advice, which can be ignored, or in the form of mandates and regulations. A simple example of that distinction is found in the various surveys that have revealed that approximately one-half of the prescriptions written by physicians are never filled and one-half of those that are filled are not used as directed. Whether that accounts for the recent increase in life expectancy is still in dispute.

The resourcing role is based on the assumption that congregational leaders can be trusted.

One of the most important changes in the American culture was discussed earlier in chapter 3. Older generations were taught to accept and respect people in positions of authority (presidents, governors, pastors, priests, police offices, professors, etc.) and to accept the authority vested in distant institutions (the federal government, denominational headquarters, the Pentagon, NASA, Congress, etc.).

Perhaps the most profound consequence of this erosion of authority in distant institutions can be seen in warfare. On July 3, 1863, that widely revered leader of the Confederate Army, Robert E. Lee, was able to order General George E. Pickett to lead what turned out to be a suicidal charge across an open field and up the slopes of Cemetery Ridge at Gettysburg. After the Confederate attack had been repelled with close to 40,000 casualties on the two sides, General Lee ordered Pickett to move his division to a new location. Pickett responded with what has become one of the famous quotations in military history: "General Lee, I have no division now."[4]

Fifty-three years later, on July 1, 1916, the British Army sent 20,000 men to their death on that first day of the Battle of the Somme in World War I.

By the 1940s, American society had become more democratic and so suspicious of centralized authority that a top priority for every general was to minimize casualties. Notable examples of such include Dwight D. Eisenhower, George Patton, and Douglas MacArthur. The American strategy for the Civil War and in World War I was dictated by the men in authority. Soldiers were perceived to be dispensable. By 1940 it was widely accepted that American diplomacy and American strategy had to be designed within the limits defined by the governed. By the time the member nations of the North Atlantic Treaty Organization (NATO) decided to launch a bombing attack on Yugoslavia in early 1999, the consent of the governed was an even more powerful political force in the United States than it had been during the Vietnam conflict thirty years earlier. President William J. Clinton was determined not to send infantry troops into Kosovo or Serbia unless he had broad popular support from the American people for such a decision. The consent of the governed was more influential than the advice of military advisers.

It is now clear that Americans born after 1940 were reared in a culture that taught distrust of authority, both individual and institutional. One consequence is the need for those in positions of authority to recognize the necessity to earn, reearn, and reearn the trust of their constituency. The trust that once went with the office has evaporated. Police officers, the clergy, physicians, teachers, and bankers are among those experiencing this change.

From a larger perspective, this is one facet of the national shift from representative democracy to participatory democracy. Once upon a time congregations were content to elect people who would go to a meeting of the regional judicatory and there elect the person who would represent them at the national denominational convention. Those representatives were empowered to adopt policies, approve goals, and make decisions that were presumed to be binding on member congregations. Most of the churchgoers born before 1940 are comfortable with that form of representative government. Most of the churchgoers born after 1950 also are comfortable with that system as long as everyone in a position of authority accepts the reservation that congregations are free to ignore any of those policies, goals, decisions, and mandates with which they disagree.

If the generations born after 1950 do outlive those born before 1940, this will have a profound impact on those religious bodies that today have an aging constituency. The generations born before 1940, and especially those born before 1928, were far more likely to affirm the policies and accept the decisions of leaders in distant institutions than are members of younger generations. Like corporate executives, government officials, managers and coaches of major league sports teams, and leaders of labor unions, denominational officials must give more weight to the consent of the governed than was the case as recently as the 1950s. Generals no longer are free to send thousands of soldiers to their death on a given day. Denominational officials can suggest or urge or advise, but they no longer can command the loyal response that was so easy to secure a few decades ago.

That generalization is especially relevant to the national leaders in the Roman Catholic Church in America, the Evangelical Lutheran Church in America, the United Methodist Church, the Episcopal Church, and the Presbyterian Church (U.S.A.). It also is especially relevant to the delegates to those national denominational conventions that meet once every one to four years to adopt a new set of rules, regulations, mandates, and directives for congregations and regional judicatories.

What Are the Alternatives?

One alternative, which appears to have been chosen by default by several denominations, is to deny that a problem exists and to continue as an increasingly dysfunctional religious tradition.

An overlapping alternative is to search for a scapegoat and focus on the rise of consumerism as the real problem. Consumerism may be the major threat to distant institutions all across American society, from network television to the delivery of health care to the design of motor vehicles to the definition of American foreign policy to the role of political parties to efforts to reverse urban sprawl to the formulation of military strategy.

A third, and by far more challenging, option is to change

the basic guiding assumption from distrust of local leaders to trust. This opens the door to redefining the denominational role from regulating to resourcing.

A fourth alternative that has considerable appeal to those nearing retirement is based on the contemporary affluence of American economy. Unlike profit-driven business, such as retail trade, commercial travel, farming, and manufacturing, non-profit organizations find it relatively easy to resist change. While they may be obsolete or irrelevant or counterproductive or dysfunctional, non-profit organizations often outlive their critics. In other words, they pass the responsibility for what may be difficult and stress-filled reforms to the next generation.

A fifth, and far more promising, alternative is to begin by defining the issue in larger terms. One example of that has been discussed earlier. Is the *primary* role of a denominational agency (1) to do ministry or (2) to regulate congregations and the clergy or (3) to resource congregations? If, and this is a big if, agreement can be reached on the conviction that a denominational agency may have two or more secondary responsibilities, but it can have only one primary role, that can be a productive approach.

If the decision is to begin by looking at the contemporary American context, as contrasted with the seventeenth- and eighteenth-century western European context, one useful introduction to contemporary American reality is Robert Wiebe's book on the history of American democracy. One of Wiebe's central themes is "centralization and hierarchy have consistently resisted the twin mandates for democratic participation." One of those two mandates is a responsive governing system.[5]

In simple either/or terms, it appears to this observer of the American political and ecclesiastical scenes that American Christianity has been experiencing two trends running in opposite directions. One is the trend in several religious traditions toward increased centralization and an expansion of the regulatory role for the leaders at head-quarters.

The opposing trend across American society has been in the direction of decentralization and an increased level of trust in the local leadership. One example of this is in the profit-driven business world. A second is in the recent rapid increase in the number of home schooling parents who choose to educate their children at home. Another is in government. A fourth is in the recent growth of nondenominational or independent congregations in which total control is vested in local leaders.

Is it only a coincidence that the religious bodies in the United States that cherish the centralization of authority and a hierarchical organizational structure also report an aging and numerically shrinking constituency, while the independent congregations are attracting a growing proportion of younger churchgoers?

Chapter Eighteen
Which Road to Multiculturalism?

The time has come for us to make a deter-mined and systematic effort to become a more inclusive denomination," declared a white executive in a predominantly white Protestant denomination.

"What do you mean by that?" asked a colleague. "What do you propose we do?"

"I propose that we try to reach a much larger number of African Americans, Asian Americans, Native Americans, and Latinos," was the immediate response.

"Does that mean you don't trust the existing black churches to reach and serve the new generations of American-born blacks?" challenged the colleague. "The last figures I saw stated there are more than 85,000 black congregations in the United States today. Do you want to undermine their ministry?"

"That thought never crossed my mind!" retorted the executive. "I am motivated by two concerns. One is to reach the tens of millions of Americans who have not made a commitment to become a disciple of Jesus Christ. The second is that we seek to reach everyone, not just those who trace all or most of their ancestry back to western Europe. That means we must become a more inclusive denomination."

The kindest words that can be used to describe that response is that it represents a well intentioned but extremely vague wish. An effective strategy will require a far greater degree of intentionality and detail plus what may be an unacceptable openness to change. There are many roads to multiculturalism. Which one is appropriate for your religious tradition?

Birds of a Feather

The most crucial single issue in developing a strategy to transform a predominantly white religious body into a multicultural denomination raises one of those "What do you believe?" questions. Do you believe that adult Americans naturally tend to relate more readily to people whom they perceive to be like themselves? This has been labeled the "homogeneous unit principle" in church growth theory. This principle declares that numerically growing congregations naturally tend to attract people who closely resemble the current membership in terms of race, nationality, language, social class, sexual orientation, theological stance, and age. The fact that birds of a particular species tend to flock together is sometimes used as a parallel.

Do you believe that represents reality? If you believe it does reflect the natural tendency of human beings, that becomes an obstacle to overcome or a barrier to be circumvented.

If you believe that principle does not reflect reality, you will design a different strategy than if you affirm the homogeneous unit principle.

A third position is held by those who concede that this principle does reflect the nature of sinful human beings, but it should not be tolerated, much less affirmed. This calls for a strategy based on how good people *should* behave, rather than on how sinful people tend to behave. Idealism becomes an influential dynamic in the planning process.

Your response to the homogeneous unit principle

becomes a highly influential factor as you select the path to take when choosing to transform a predominantly white denomination into a multicultural religious body.

Separatist or Integrationist?

The second "What do you believe?" question was introduced earlier in the fourth chapter. What do you believe is the stronger motivating force among American Christians who carry an ethnic minority heritage? When it comes to participating in a worshiping community, which is a far different issue than the workplace or the school house or the hospital or the motion picture theater or the restaurant or the city bus or a political party, what is their preference? Ethnic integration? Or ethnic separation?

The predominantly white denomination will find the road to becoming a truly multicultural religious body will be relatively steep if the focus is on reaching the separatists. As your denomination seeks to reach and serve African Americans, Chinese Americans, Native Americans, Mexican Americans, and members of other ethnic minority groups, will that effort be directed at integrationists? Or separatists? Or both?

What Is Fair?

The third question is, Do you believe the concept of the "American melting pot" requires the rapid and full assimilation of all ethnic minority groups into a predominantly white American culture? Or do you believe the dream of full self-determination affirms the concept of an all-black college or an all-Korean theological school, or an all-Taiwanese congregation or an all-black denomination?

In a culture built largely on a western European heritage, is the first principle in your system of justice the greatest good for the greatest number? Or is the first principle in

199

your system of justice the greatest good for the most disadvantaged?

In simple terms, in a demographically diverse and ideologically pluralistic culture dominated by white persons with a western European ancestry, do you believe members of ethnic minority groups have two rights, (a) the right to equal access to full and equal membership in predominantly white institutions and (b) the right to create and control monocultural private institutions such as lodges, elementary schools, newspapers, radio stations, television networks, colleges, churches, and theological schools?

The First Fork in the Road

If the goal is to become a multicultural religious body, then experience suggests that the easiest strategy to implement is to become a multicultural denomination composed of a collection of monocultural and self-governing smaller units. An outstanding contemporary example is The Christian and Missionary Alliance (CM&A), which traces its origins back to 1887 and the initiative of a Presbyterian minister, Dr. Albert B. Simpson.

The two thousand congregations in the United States are divided among twenty-two regional districts defined in geographical terms plus eleven ethnic minority nongeographical districts (three Spanish, two Haitian, one each Hmong, Korean, Laotian, Native American, Cambodian, and Vietnamese). The federalist system allows ethnic minority congregations to belong to an ethnic minority district or to a predominantly Anglo district or to an ethnic minority association within a geographically defined district.

The CM&A, therefore, is an excellent model of creating a multicultural religious body within a network of what are largely monocultural congregations.

It must be added, however, that the CM&A enjoys four advantages over most "made-in-America" denominations.

By far the most important advantage is that it was organized to fulfill the Great Commission, which continues to be the central organizing and unifying principle more than a century later! Unlike for many other Protestant denominations, that central organizing principle has not been diluted by other issues.

At various times most other American denominations have been disrupted by internal quarrels over biblical interpretation, doctrine, power, ecumenism, social justice issues, maintaining relationships with aging institutions founded by white males who have been dead for many decades, sex, abortion, divorce, racial justice, American foreign policy, the elimination of poverty, and economic concerns.

Throughout American church history, the only unifying issue in denominational circles has been to implement the Great Commission. All other organizing principles, such as polity, doctrine, biblical interpretation, and ecumenism, turn out to be divisive. Each encourages a "choose up sides" response. By seeing itself as a movement that exists to fulfill the Great Commission, the CM&A has been largely immune to these divisive internal battles.

A second advantage enjoyed by the CM&A is a relatively narrow focus in its world missionary efforts. The central focus has been (a) to plant new missions and (b) to identify, enlist, challenge, equip, and place indigenous leaders in these congregations. One expression of the first emphasis is that the CM&A includes twice as many congregations in the Philippines, Indonesia, and South Korea (combined) as in the United States. CM&A congregations in all parts of the world outnumber those in the United States by a nine to two ratio.

The second emphasis on trained indigenous leadership is illustrated by the existence of more than one hundred theological schools in other parts of the world with more than ten thousand students.

One consequence is that recent immigration into the United States includes thousands of CM&A church members and CM&A ministers. This helps to explain why the majority of new CM&A missions in the United States are ethnic minority congregations. The indigenous pastors and the core constituencies are here. Those denominations that placed a high priority in their missionary endeavors on founding hospitals, schools, homes, and training centers do not enjoy this advantage.

While of lesser importance, a third advantage possessed by the CM&A is the ratio of one career U.S. missionary for every 3.5 U.S. congregations. That makes it relatively easy for most American church members to comprehend that central organizing principle. The CM&A exists to fulfill the Great Commission!

The big intangible advantage of the CM&A can be summarized in the word passion. The leaders and missionaries do not perceive missions as a duty or an obligation or a heritage. The CM&A is organized around a passion for evangelism. That explains why the CM&A often placed a high priority on the most hard to reach populations in the most obscure, and often dangerous, locations.

Caution: Lest these comments about The Christian and Missionary Alliance be perceived as a description of the perfect multicultural system, it should be noted that a task force has been appointed to study the district organizational design. It is impossible to design a denominational structure that will meet all needs and make everyone happy!

That point can be illustrated by a brief look at an earlier model built on federalism.

During the 1920s the Methodist Episcopal Church, one of the six predecessor bodies of what is now The United Methodist Church, included ten German conferences, six Swedish conferences, two Norwegian-Danish conferences, twenty African American conferences, two Hispanic conferences, one Japanese conference, and one Chinese conference plus the white geographical annual conferences. The goal was to function as a multinational and multicultural denomination composed of monoracial and mononational annual conferences that were collections of largely mononational congregations. The federalist organizational system described in chapter 2 was used to design the denominational system. This was abandoned in the middle third of the twentieth century in favor of a highly centralized system that replaced the old affirmation of diversity with a new emphasis on denomination-wide uniformity.

Multicultural Judicatories

A second road requires a shifting of the focus from the national body to the smaller subunits. This strategy calls for the creation of a multicultural denomination consisting of a collection of smaller multicultural units (dioceses, synods, conferences, districts, etc.), each of which includes a large number of congregations, most of which are either monocultural or bicultural. For example, a district might include thirty predominantly Anglo congregations, twenty that are predominantly American-born blacks, two that are African- or Caribbean-born blacks, four Korean churches, three Mexican American, one where most of the members trace their ancestry back to Colombia, six that consist largely of self-identified Americans of Mexican ancestry but with a growing number of members who trace their ancestry to western Europe, two that are racially integrated, three Chinese American congregations, one composed largely of immigrants from the Gujarati section of India, one Native American congregation, and two consisting largely of the American-born adult children of Korean immigrant parents and their spouses, many of whom are either Anglo or Hispanic.

That multicultural regional judicatory is composed, for the most part, of monocultural congregations.

203

The Uphill Road

A third, and perhaps the steepest uphill road, is to create a multicultural denomination consisting of multicultural regional judicatories that are collections of multicultural congregations. The driving force in this strategy is for every congregation to be a multicultural church—or at least a bicultural parish.

The obvious reason why this is such a difficult-to-implement strategy is that it runs counter to the homogeneous unit principle. A second reason is that it places a heavy burden on the pastor. Few pastors in the predominantly white Protestant denominations have the benefit of either the training or the experience to be comfortable in a multicultural congregation. One exception is the adult child of Anglo missionaries to Korea or Mexico or China or India or Vietnam who was born, reared, and educated in that country. This young candidate for the ministry next graduates from a theological school in Canada or India or the United States or Mexico and subsequently goes out to serve as the pastor of a bicultural or multicultural congregation.

Relatively few American-born ministers with a western European ancestry are comfortable and fluent in two or three languages plus English.

A third factor is that most of the predominantly white Protestant denominations are composed largely of Anglo congregations founded before 1960. The guiding principle is that it is easier to create the new than to change the old.

Therefore, if the goal is to create a network of multicultural congregations, a high priority should be given to planting new missions that are multicultural—or at least bicultural—communities from their very beginning. A reasonable goal would be to double the number of congregations in ten years so that within a decade a majority of congregations are at least bicultural. That is an awesome goal when one recognizes the tremendous pressures on denominational policy makers to keep the dying alive rather than to create the new.

Highly Visible Minority Leadership

One of the most attractive roads to multiculturalism is to change the criteria for selecting denominational leaders. The old system filled most leadership positions with mature white males. The new systems are designed with the hope that selecting leaders from heretofore excluded groups will demonstrate the desire for this to become a more inclusive religious body. The high visibility of these leaders will send a signal to those who have felt excluded that they are now welcome. A major fringe benefit is that the policymaking process will benefit from the insights of women, youth, blacks, Asians, Native Americans, Latinos, and other minority groups.

While it is (a) premature to offer a final evaluation of this strategy and (b) impossible to prove a cause-and-effect relationship, it appears that the number-one success story is in reaching and retaining more women. Several denominations that formerly reported their membership was approximately 53 percent female and 47 percent male (the current distribution by gender of the adult population in the United States) now report that over 60 percent of their adult members are female. Filling more of the highly visible leadership positions with women can be an effective tactic in a larger strategy to encourage more women to consider the professional ministry as a vocation.

What Is Working?

The pragmatists who want to transform a predominantly white Protestant denomination may begin by asking,

"What's working? What is the crucial variable in those existing congregations that are multicultural religious bodies?"

One answer can be found in what are often described as high-expectation churches. Their strategy often includes (1) offering an unreserved welcome to everyone who wants to worship here; (2) projecting clear expectations of those who want to become more involved as participants in Bible study, prayer ministries, outreach efforts, etc.; (3) providing a carefully designed path to help believers become learners and to transform learners into disciples; (4) projecting very high expectations of anyone seeking to become a full member; and (5) designing meaningful training programs for those who want to be engaged in volunteer ministries or as volunteer leaders. This model usually requires pastorates of twenty to forty years.

The Multisite Option

The easiest strategy for the predominantly Anglo congregation to implement calls for the creation of off-campus worshiping communities. Instead of inviting members of ethnic minority groups to "Come join us on our turf and learn to do what we do and how we do it," this strategy calls for enlisting and training volunteer lay ministers to go out and create new off-campus ministries that gather either on neutral turf or on the home turf of this new constituency. These groups could include recent immigrants from Vietnam, recent immigrants from Cambodia, single-parent mothers, recent newcomers from Mexico, upper-middle-class college graduates in their mid-twenties, and well-educated recent immigrants from Nigeria.

A major asset in implementing this design is a minister of missions (who may be part-time or a volunteer) who is driven by a passion for evangelism and also is effective in enlisting, training, placing, and supporting teams of volunteers.

The Charismatic Renewal Movement

A parallel to the high-expectation church illustrates a road that has been taken by a very large number of multicultural congregations. These churches rely on an ancient Christian principle of building on a point of commonality that overrides differences based on race, income, language, gender, nationality, social class, education, age, marital status, or vocation. Most of the high-expectation churches rely on discipleship as that point of commonality. By definition, every member is a fully committed and trained disciple of Jesus Christ engaged in volunteer ministry. That line of demarcation, rather than nationality or race or social class, is what distinguishes the members from that larger number who are simply worshipers.

In another group of multicultural congregations, that point of commonality is the baptism of the Holy Spirit and the receipt of a clearly identifiable spiritual gift. By definition, all members are charismatic Christians, and that is a far more significant part of one's identity than race, gender, nationality, social class, income, age, occupation, marital status, education, income, or competence in the English language.

A basic generalization is that the stronger that point of commonality, the less likely that multicultural quality will be eroded when the current pastor eventually departs.

The Multicultural Leadership Team

A small but growing number of long-established and predominantly Anglo congregations have become multicultural churches by choosing a road that reflects a contemporary secular trend (see chap. 15). This alternative calls for a pastor in an intercultural marriage plus two or more program staff members from other ethnic minority heritages. This model also requires a high degree of patience, since the persuasive measurable results seldom surface before year five or six of that pastorate. Ideally that three-person staff team will work together for at least a decade.

The Common Cause

While it is far from easy, an eighth road was illustrated in chapter 4. Go into a multicultural community and identify a widely shared point of frustration and concern that a Christian congregation can address. Organize and staff a new mission that provides the skills and capability to rally residents to respond to that challenge. The driving force is not to create a multicultural congregation. That should be seen as a fringe benefit, rather than as the central goal.

This design is much easier to implement in a new congregation than in one that has been in existence for a decade or more. It also is far easier to implement if the focus is on one cause rather than on a collection of ideologically divisive goals.

Marriage Vows to Multiculturalism

The newest rapidly widening road to building multicultural congregations is the product of recent changes in marriage patterns. Once upon a time Germans married Germans, African Americans married African Americans, Catholics married Catholics, Koreans married Koreans, Jews married Jews, Puerto Ricans married Puerto Ricans, Lutherans married Lutherans, and Baptists married Baptists. Today one out of ten African American men who marry choose a bride who does not come from an African ancestry. One-fourth of American-born women of Asian ancestry who marry choose a husband who does not come from an Asian ancestry. Nearly one-third of foreign-born married women in the United States whose native language was Spanish and who were born in the 1975–84 era are married to a husband who is of European or Asian or African descent. A rapidly growing proportion of brides and bridegrooms with European ancestors choose a mate from a different cultural heritage. The young golfer Tiger Woods is a symbol of that new era.

One result is the intercultural couple who want to demonstrate to their children that they represent the new norm in American society, not an aberration. One way to communicate that lesson to their children is to find a church that includes many couples in an intercultural marriage.

The Christian Day School

One of the oldest and most effective ways for the largely Anglo urban congregation to reach American-born black families has been and continues to be the Christian day school. A crucial distinction in this strategy is between the perception of the school as a community service project and the school as one component of a larger package of ministries with families with young children. The Lutheran Church-Missouri Synod, the Roman Catholic Church, the Seventh-Day Adventist Church, and the Episcopal Church are among those that have implemented this strategy most effectively.

Adopt

If your denominational polity permits this, a relatively easy road to multiculturalism is dual affiliation. This is a "both/and" strategy designed to encourage the affiliation of ethnic minority churches that also retain their membership in their ethnic or nationality denomination. Thus, for example, one congregation can be affiliated with both the Progressive National Baptist Convention, Inc., and with a predominantly Anglo denomination.

Paralleling this is the growing number of immigrant

congregations that began as independent or nondenominational churches and subsequently affiliated with a Euro-American denomination. For example, what originally was an independent Korean congregation is now a full member of The United Methodist Church.

For those who place equity above easing white guilt in their hierarchy of values, two radically different alternatives merit consideration. These are derived from the fact that for generations blacks in America have been expected to fit into a predominantly white culture. Blacks have been expected to fit into the white culture in the public schools, in the criminal justice system, in a largely white controlled labor force, in white controlled institutions of higher education (with a few notable exceptions), in white controlled systems of health care, in white controlled political parties, and in the white controlled media. Among the few exceptions are the black lodges, the black churches, the black colleges, and a shrinking number of black newspapers.

Rather than expect American-born blacks to join what are largely white controlled religious bodies, another road to becoming a biracial religious body calls for the predominantly white denomination to merge into a black denomination and adapt to the culture of that black religious tradition. This probably would mean that a large proportion of the congregations in the white denomination would choose to create a new denomination rather than participate in that merger. It also probably would produce a gradual departure of many of the black congregations who would be uncomfortable with the increasing number of whites moving into leadership positions in the new denomination.

A reality check suggests that the current leaders, both white and black, in the predominantly white denominations would be reluctant to surrender the power they have enjoyed and, therefore, would be unlikely to aggressively promote such mergers. How many predominantly white denominations want to be adopted and assimilated into a predominantly African American or Korean or Chinese denomination?

That denominational barrier introduces another road to multiculturalism. This road affirms congregational autonomy and assumes that it is better to choose what the people want than to impose what a small number of leaders believe the people want.

This strategy calls for the voluntary union of what have been largely or entirely monocultural congregations. Thus a predominantly white congregation could merge with a Latino church and a black congregation. Or an upper-middle-class Korean congregation could merge with an upper-middle-class Spanish-language church and an upper-middle-class Anglo parish.

Instead of language, race, culture, and nationality being lines of demarcation, the focus could be on points of commonality, such as social class, education, upward mobility ambitions for the children, a shared theological position, and a common ideological stance on social and political issues.

Reform the Old or Create the New?

Finally, for those who place the dream of a multicultural denomination composed of multicultural congregations at the top of their wish list, the only guaranteed road to making that wish become a reality is to create a new multicultural movement or denomination. The one non-negotiable requirement for a congregation to become a member of this new denomination would be that (a) no more than 50 percent of the current members could come from any one racial, nationality, language, or ethnic group (thus two monocultural congregations could be motivated to merge in order to qualify for membership in this new body); (b) at least 25 percent of the members represent a second ethnic

211

heritage; and (c) at least 5 percent represent a third ethnic heritage.

The three sources for membership would be (a) existing multicultural congregations, (b) new multicultural missions that attract people who place a high value on being members of a multicultural religious body, and (c) those newly merged congregations that are now multicultural.

Those who consider this last road to be the product of hallucinatory drugs or senility or a mental impairment need to be reminded that a similar dynamic has produced more than five hundred of the Christian religious bodies in the United States today. The typical sequence began with a small number of Christians who became increasingly discontented with their denominational system. Eventually they were confronted with three choices: (a) reform their denomination, (b) transfer their loyalty to another religious tradition, or (c) leave and organize a new religious body. The third appeared to be the most attractive, and perhaps the easiest, choice.

A Wish or a Goal?

Several of the alternatives presented here, and especially the last three, can be used to illustrate the difference between a wish and a goal. A wish is a passive statement by someone that does not require any initiative or effort by the one making the wish. For example, I wish I weighed twenty pounds less than my current weight. That is a sincere wish!

By contrast, a goal usually requires sacrifice. To transform my wish into a goal requires an action plan. That may be eating less. It may mean more physical exercise. It may mean eating what I do not like and forgoing what I enjoy eating. Purchasing a book on losing weight does not fit that definition of sacrifice.

Likewise, transforming a predominantly Anglo denomination derived from a western European religious heritage into a multicultural religious body will require sacrifice. ~~The predominantly Anglo congregation that wishes it~~ were ~~a multicultural church also must make sacrifices~~ if it ~~decides to replace that wish with an attainable goal.~~

The most widespread illustration of this distinction between a wish and a goal is the hundred-year-old white congregation with what today is an aging and shrinking membership. The number-one wish is for a young pastor who could attract large numbers of young couples with children at home. Turning that wish into an attainable goal may require many changes that the old-timers will evaluate as unacceptable sacrifices.

Four Questions

1. Is your denomination interested in becoming a multi-cultural religious body?

2. If yes, what is the strategy to turn that wish into an attainable goal? Which of the paths to multiculturalism described here will your denomination follow? (If the answer is, "All of them," that probably represents the absence of a carefully defined and internally consistent strategy.)

3. What changes and sacrifices will be required to turn that wish into reality?

4. Where does your congregation fit into that larger denominational strategy?

NOTES

Introduction

1. Robert W. Fogel, *The Fourth Great Awakening* (Chicago: University of Chicago Press, 2000), 15-43.

2. For a provocative discussion of the changing role of the parish priest in the Roman Catholic Church in the United States, see Donald B. Cozzens, *The Changing Face of the Priesthood* (Collegeville, Minn.: The Liturgical Press, 2000). Cozzens points out that the clerical culture of the Roman Catholic Church tends to reward docility and compliance. He also lifts up the shift from the remoteness of the priest from the laity in the old ecclesiastical culture to the emphasis on commonality with other church members in the contemporary world. He repeatedly identifies the conflict that is a product of the battle between traditions and data based on contemporary reality. One product of that conflict is denial. Another is alienation. A third is irrelevance. The Protestant culture and the Roman Catholic culture do have much in common!

1. What Happened?

1. For a more detailed analysis of the impact of decentralization, see Lyle E. Schaller, *Discontinuity and Hope* (Nashville: Abingdon Press, 1999), 74-81.

2. Will Herberg, *Protestant-Catholic-Jew* (Garden City, N.Y.: Doubleday, 1956).

3. For a brief review of the evolution of comity, see Lyle E. Schaller, *The Small Membership Church* (Nashville: Abingdon Press, 1994), 59-77.

4. A comprehensive mid-stages introduction to the church growth movement is C. Peter Wagner, ed., *Church Growth: State of the Art* (Wheaton, Ill.: Tyndale House, 1986).

2. Uniformity or Diversity?

1. Suggestions for tactics on planned change can be found in Lyle E. Schaller, *Strategies for Change* (Nashville: Abingdon Press, 1993), 90-106.

2. The multisite option is discussed by Lyle E. Schaller, *Innovations in Ministry* (Nashville: Abingdon Press, 1994), 86-133.
3. The Key Church Strategy is described in J. Timothy Ahlen and J. V. Thomas, *One Church, Many Congregations* (Nashville: Abingdon Press, 1999).

3. What Will They Want Next?

1. For this observer's earlier views on community organizing strategies, see Lyle E. Schaller, *Community Organization* (Nashville: Abingdon Press, 1966).

6. From Law to Grace

1. Four excellent books that describe what has been happening along that theological spectrum are Christian Smith, *American Evangelicalism* (Chicago: University of Chicago Press, 1998); Joel A. Carpenter, *Revive Us Again* (New York: Oxford University Press, 1997); Donald E. Miller, *Reinventing American Protestantism* (Berkeley: University of California Press, 1997); and R. Stephen Warner, *New Wine in Old Wineskins* (Berkeley: University of California Press, 1988). It is interesting to note that all four of these were published by university presses, as was Robert W. Fogel, *The Fourth Great Awakening* (Chicago: University of Chicago Press, 2000). See note to Introduction.

7. From Obligation to Adventure and Excitemenst

1. Daniel Roth, "My Job at the Container Center," *Fortune*, January 10, 2000, 74-76. Jerry Useem, "Welcome to the New Company Town," *Fortune*, (January 10, 2000, 62-70.
2. John Seabrook, "Selling the Weather," *The New Yorker*, April 3, 2000, 44-53.
3. Ronald Steel, "Brackish Beach," *The New Republic*, December 6, 1999, 42.
4. The possibility that learning can be challenging and enjoyable, and need not be boring, is a central theme of Lyle E. Schaller, *The Evolution of the American Public High School: From Prep School to Prison to Partnerships* (Nashville: Abingdon Press, 2000).

8. It Is a More Competitive World!

1. The impact of consumerism on the churches is discussed at greater length in Lyle E. Schaller, *The Very Large Church* (Nashville: Abingdon Press, 2000), 76-106.
2. Several reasons for the shortage of large Protestant congregations are identified in Ibid., 107-36.

9. Income or Wealth?

1. *The Chronicle of Higher Education* (October 15, 1999): A43.
2. Kit Lively, "Giving to Higher Education Breaks Another Record," *The Chronicle of Higher Education* (May 5, 2000): A41.
3. W. Fred Smith, Jr., "The Present and Future of Religious Giving," an address to the Philanthropy Roundtable Panel (October 29, 1999).

13. What Is the Role of Music?

1. Bobby Horton, foreword to *Singing the New Nation: How Music Shaped the Confederacy, 1816-1865*, by E. Lawrence Abel (Mechanicsburg, Pa.: Stackpole Books, 2000), VI.
2. For resources on music- and movement-based learning, contact Early Childhood Connections Foundation For Music-Based Learning, P. O. Box 4274, Greensboro, NC 27404-4274.

14. What Will the World Wide Web Bring?

1. Tim Berness-Lee, *Weaving the Web* (San Francisco: Harper San Francisco, 1999).
2. Benjamin M. Friedman, "The Power of the Elecronic Herd," *The New York Review of Books*, July 15, 1999, 40.

15. From the Wedding Business to a Marriage Ministry

1. See note 2 to chapter 13.
2. For an excellent review of the married life of the baby boom generation in the United States in the 1950s, see Jessica Weiss, *To Have and to Hold* (Chicago: The University of Chicago Press, 2000).

16. How Do You Classify Churches?

1. Will Herberg, *Protestant-Catholic-Jew* (Garden City, N.Y.: Doubleday, 1956).

2. For the curious, 44 is the smallest number that can be divided evenly by 1, 2, 4, and 11. One plus two plus four equals seven. Therefore, 44 represents two interesting numbers: 7 and 11. Do you regret you asked?

3. A conceptual framework for using average worship attendance as a system for classifying congregations is presented in Lyle E. Schaller, *Looking in the Mirror* (Nashville: Abingdon Press, 1984), 14-37.

4. This concept of the multisite congregation is described in Lyle E. Schaller, *Innovations in Ministry* (Nashville: Abingdon Press, 1994), 86-133; and J. Timothy Ahlen and J. V. Thomas, *One Church, Many Congregations* (Nashville: Abingdon Press, 1999).

17. Who Resources Whom?

1. For a pioneering essay on the natural tendency of a denomination to drift into a regulatory role, see Craig Dyskra and James Hudnut-Beumler, "The National Organizational Structures of Protestant Denominations," in *The Organizational Revolution*, ed. Milton J. Coulter et al. (Louisville: Westminster/John Knox Press, 1992), 307-31.

2. Twenty of the estimated 1,200 different religious traditions in the United States account for 260,000 of the estimated 375,000 Christian congregations.

3. For a more extended discussion on the issue of trust, see Lyle E. Schaller, *Tattered Trust* (Nashville: Abingdon Press, 1996).

4. Richard Harwell, *Lee: An Abridgement of R. E. Lee* by Douglas Southall Freeman (New York: Charles Scribner's Sons, 1961) 341.

5. Robert H. Wiebe, *Self-Rule: A Cultural History of American Democracy* (Chicago: University of Chicago Press, 1995), 253.